Excel

Get the Results You Want!

YEARS
5–8

AGES
10–14

WRITER'S HANDBOOK

Phil Walker

PASCAL PRESS

Reprinted 2011, 2014, 2017, 2019, 2021, 2022

ISBN 978 1 74125 283 5

Pascal Press
PO Box 250
Glebe NSW 2037
(02) 8585 4050
www.pascalpress.com.au

Publisher: Vivienne Joannou
Project editor: Mark Dixon
Edited by Christine Eslick
Typeset by Julianne Billington
Portrait of John Forrest, 1874, nla.pic-an23382380; reproduced with permission of the National Library of Australia
Photo of Ian Thorpe by Corbis
Cover by DiZign Pty Ltd
Printed by Vivar Printing/Green Giant Press

Contents

Introduction v

Part A: Focus on developing your writing

1 How to write narrative and factual texts 1
- Narrative texts 2
- Factual texts 10

2 Making and using notes 14

3 Examining a topic 24
- Describe 25
- Discuss 27
- Narrate 29
- Compare 31
- Summarise 34

4 Punctuation and writing conventions 37
- Capitals and full stops 38
- Commas, question marks and exclamation marks 40
- Apostrophes, colons and semicolons 42
- Hyphens, dashes and brackets 44
- Numbers, measurements, dates and times 46
- Abbreviations, contractions and acronyms 48
- Direct and indirect speech—quotation marks 50

Part B: Focus on improving your writing

5 Writing better sentences 53
- Adding adjectives and adjectival phrases 54
- Adding adverbs and adverbial phrases 55
- Adding participle and verbal noun phrases 57
- Adding infinitive phrases 58
- Adding adjectival and adverbial clauses 59
- Sentence variety 61
- Changing sentence form 62
- Avoiding repetition 63

6 Paragraphs 68

Reorganising paragraphs	70
Sequence of paragraphs	72
Topic sentences and main ideas	73
Identifying main ideas and supporting details	77
Rules for paragraphs	83
Paragraphs in dialogue	84

7 Setting a scene 85

Using general and specific names	87
Adding adjectives	90
Using expressive verbs	92
Adding time and place	95

8 Creating word pictures 101

Appealing to the senses	102
Including feelings and emotions	106
Using similes and metaphors	108
Creating real people—describing appearance	109
Creating real people—expressions and attitudes	110
Descriptive scenes	114
Descriptive scenes—time order	115

Part C: Focus on constructing texts

9 Text types 116

Procedures	117
Discussions	121
Explanations	124
Expositions	127
Information reports	130
Recounts—factual	134
Recounts—literary	137
Descriptions	139
Responses	141
Responses—reviews	143
Narratives	145
Poetry	147

Answers 150

Introduction

The ***Excel*** **Writer's Handbook** is a comprehensive guide to improving a student's writing. The book is in three sections:

- Part A Focus on developing your writing
- Part B Focus on improving your writing
- Part C Focus on constructing texts

Each section consists of introductory explanatory material, examples and activities related to each chapter topic.

The main focus of each section is on providing a sound base for developing writing skills by the study of various explanations and examples. The remainder of each chapter provides structured activities.

These structured activities, graduated in complexity, provide opportunities for students to practise the many aspects of writing and text construction.

The workbook layout will prove valuable to the following groups of students:

- **students in Years 5–8** requiring a comprehensive coverage of writing skills and opportunities to practise practical activities to develop and enhance their writing
- **students from a non–English speaking background** who would benefit from a comprehensive and easy-to-follow course in writing skills.

Answers and explanations (where necessary) have been included for self-assessment.

Part A Focus on developing your writing

In these chapters you will look at how to develop your ideas so that you can write all types of literary and factual texts. You will learn ways to organise your writing so that it is logical and easy to follow.

1 How to write narrative and factual texts

In this chapter you will focus on the **steps** you can follow to write texts.

Texts fall into **two groups**: literary texts and factual texts. They include the following types of writing.

Literary texts (narratives)

drama	fantasy	myths	scripts for radio, television or film
verse	fables	legends	historical narratives
ballads	folk tales	science fiction	fairytales

Factual texts

discussion	information reports	explanation	exposition
procedures	news articles	documentaries	editorials
interviews	letters	recounts	

Steps to develop a piece of writing

To develop your piece of writing requires the following five steps.

1 Brainstorming

Think of a scene or incident to create a basic outline and then expand on it by exploring ideas in many directions. As you jot down these rough ideas, the structure of your piece of writing may emerge. This is the final outline.

2 Drafting

Expand the final outline to complete the piece of writing. Add interesting words, phrases and clauses to create a convincing and interesting piece of writing.

3 Format and sequence checking

Check over the format and sequence to make sure the writing flows smoothly from one scene or incident to another.

4 Reviewing and editing

Check sentence construction, grammar, spelling and punctuation. In addition, pay attention to those sentences that could be written in more expressive and interesting ways.

5 Presenting/publishing

After completing the previous step, present the final work in an easy to read and attractive layout.

Narrative texts

Task

Jenny's task was to write a narrative about an incident in a rural area.
She chose *Bushfire danger* as her topic.

Step 1 Brainstorming

Jenny began her preparation by writing a basic outline (four or five lines). She used questions beginning with **who**, **where**, **when**, **why** and **what** to give herself a start.

Who?	**Characters for narrative**	Helen Dyer, brother Jason
When?	**Time of incident**	Summer
Where?	**Location of incident**	Outside township of Mt Alford
Why?	**How did the incident begin?**	Lightning strike
What?	**What danger did the bushfire cause?**	Danger to livestock and buildings

Jenny's basic outline

Last summer — Helen and Jason Dyer — outside township of Mt Alford — severe bushfire — caused by lightning strike — danger to livestock and buildings

Jenny read over her basic outline and decided to add more detail to it. Again the Five Ws are useful starting points.

- **Who** were Helen and Jason visiting?
- **Why** were Helen and Jason visiting?
- **What** did the two enjoy on the property?
- **What** type of property were they living on?
- **What** were weather conditions like when they arrived?
- **Where** did the fire start?
- **Why** did it advance so rapidly?
- **What** actions did the family take?
- **What** was the final result?

By using these questions Jenny was able to add to her basic outline.

Jenny's final outline

Last summer — Helen and Jason Dyer — visitors — family friends — Joe and Elaine Tanty — children — Liz and Gary — always enjoyed horse riding — mustering cattle — trail bike riding — cattle property — over two thousand hectares — long drought conditions — very hot and dry southern ridge — first sign of smoke — gusting — westerly winds — small water truck — pump and hoses — bags battled fire on ridge — down into valley — cattle almost surrounded — long struggle — finally winds dropped five hours — exhausted — livestock and buildings safe

Narrative texts

Step 2 Drafting

Jenny then used her final outline to **complete** the **narrative**.

- The outline provides the framework of the narrative.
- At this point the writer is **adding to** the **outline**, constructing expressive sentences and using interesting phrases and clauses to bring the narrative to life.
- Sometimes a writer may **alter part** of the outline to make the narrative more convincing or interesting.
- When drafting your writing it is best to **leave spaces** between lines and at the beginning and end of lines so that corrections and additions can be made. If you are using an exercise book, write on every second line.

Jenny's first draft

Bushfire danger

Last summer Helen and Jason Dyer's parents told the children that they could spend two weeks at their friend's property. The two children were very excited as they always enjoyed a visit. Joe and Elaine Tanty had been their parent's best friends for many years. Helen and Jason also enjoyed being with Joe and Elaine's children, Liz and Gary. Horse riding, mustering cattle and trail bike riding on their 2000 hectare property were always exciting.

The weather had been verry hot and the property was dry. On the second day at the homestead the wind increased in strength and by the third day a hot westerly wind was blowing. During the early hours of the third day there was a fierce electrical storm. There was hardly a drop of rain but spectacular lightning flashed across the sky. Elaine was the first to notice the smoke.

A small, dense cloud of smoke was moving from the western ridge. Action was needed at once. Joe and Elaine had a small water tanker and with all aboard they crossed the paddocks to the western ridge as fast as the ancient tanker would take them. By this time the fire had extended to both left and right and was moving slowly down the western ridge.

Elaine soon had the fire hose on the centre section of the fire, while Joe and the children using wet bags tried to contain the fire spreading slowly to left and right. While the tanker and main hose were stopping the fire in the centre it was spreading out left and right and threatened to surround the cattle in the western paddock. The dry grass burnt easily and it was a tiring task. Fortunately the winds had dropped somewhat otherwise the livestock would have been in a dangerous position.

Several hours went by and the heat and effort were wearing down the adults and the children. To the left and right the fire soon reached an almost bare piece of ground. This was the break the fire fighters needed. With a last strenuous effort the centre section was extinguished and the left and right sections were under control. Joe and Elaine were greatly relieved as the situation was now safe.

Although very tired and blackened by the ash and smoke they stood and watched the last of the flames die out.

It had been an exciting day for Helen and Jason but they never realised the difficulties faced by firefighters and though exhausted they were quite proud of their efforts.

Narrative texts

Step 3 **Format and sequence checking**

Jenny then checked that the **format**, or structure, of the work was appropriate.

- There is no standard format for narratives but it is important that the **text flows easily** from **one scene to another**.
- New paragraphs are used for **time, setting** and **action changes**.

Jenny noted that her work included the **essential aspects** of a **narrative**:

- orientation
- complication
- resolution
- coda.

Orientation: setting the scene, the time, the characters, the place
Complication: the sequence of events that causes a problem for the main characters or others
Resolution: the detail that explains how the complication is resolved (the result of some action)
Coda: an optional aspect that identifies any discoveries or learnings that the incident has provided for the main characters or others in the narrative.

Step 4 **Reviewing and editing**

Jenny then checked the narrative for **mistakes** and **poor expression**.

- The narrative has to be read carefully to check that there is nothing that is **difficult to understand**.
- There should be no errors in **sentence construction**, **spelling**, **grammar** or **punctuation**.
- **Sentences** should be looked at carefully in case they are **incomplete** or **too long** to be understood easily.
- In this step consider the way the thoughts are expressed. Are there more **expressive** and **interesting ways** to convey the meaning?

In Jenny's reviewed and edited draft, the errors she corrected and the changes she thought were needed are shown underlined. Compare these sections with her first draft.

Narrative texts

Jenny's reviewed and edited draft

Bushfire danger

Last summer, the parents of Helen and Jason Dyer told them that they could spend two weeks at their friends' property near Mt Alford. The two children were very excited as they always enjoyed a visit. Joe and Elaine Tanty had been their parents' best friends for many years. Helen and Jason also enjoyed being with Joe and Elaine's children, Liz and Gary. Horse riding, mustering cattle and trail bike riding on the Tanty's 2000 hectare property were always exciting.

The weather had been very hot and the property was tinder dry. On the second day at the homestead the wind increased in strength and by the third day a hot westerly wind was blowing. During the early hours of the third day there was a fierce electrical storm. There was hardly a drop of rain but spectacular lightning flashed across the sky.

Elaine was the first to notice the smoke. A small, dense cloud of smoke was moving from the western ridge. Action was needed at once. Joe and Elaine had a small water tanker and with all the children aboard they crossed the paddocks to the western ridge as fast as the ancient tanker would take them. By this time the fire had extended to both the left- and right-hand sides of the slope and was moving slowly down the western ridge.

Elaine soon had the fire hose on the centre section of the fire, while Joe and the children, using wet bags, tried to contain the fire spreading rapidly to left and right. While the tanker and main hose were stopping the fire in the centre, the blaze was spreading out left and right and threatened to surround the cattle in the western paddock. The dry grass burnt easily and it was a tiring task. Fortunately the winds had dropped somewhat, otherwise the livestock would have been in a dangerous position.

Several hours went by and the heat and effort were wearing down both adults and children. To the left and right the fire soon reached an almost bare piece of ground. This was the break the fire fighters needed. With a last, strenuous effort, the centre section was extinguished and the left and right sections were brought under control.

Joe and Elaine were greatly relieved as the situation was now safe. Although very tired and blackened by the ash and smoke they stood and watched the last of the flames die out.

It had been an exciting day for Helen and Jason but they never before realised the difficulties faced by fire fighters. Though exhausted, they were quite proud of their efforts and knew they had an interesting adventure to tell their parents on their return to the city.

Narrative texts

Step 5 **Presenting/publishing**

Jenny's work was now ready for the last stage. The first four steps had ensured that the finished work was easy to read, free from spelling, punctuation and grammatical errors, and sequenced correctly.

Jenny now decided that she would **publish** the work on her computer.

- She selected a suitable **simple font** that was easy to read.
- She spaced the work out well, leaving a **line between** each of the **paragraphs**.

Jenny's final draft

Bushfire danger

Last summer, the parents of Helen and Jason Dyer told them that they could spend two weeks at their friends' property near Mt Alford. The two children were very excited as they always enjoyed a visit. Joe and Elaine Tanty had been their parents' best friends for many years. Helen and Jason also enjoyed being with Joe and Elaine's children, Liz and Gary. Horse riding, mustering cattle and trail bike riding on the Tanty's 2000 hectare property were always exciting.

The weather had been very hot and the property was tinder dry. On the second day at the homestead the wind increased in strength and by the third day a hot westerly wind was blowing. During the early hours of the third day there was a fierce electrical storm. There was hardly a drop of rain but spectacular lightning flashed across the sky.

Elaine was the first to notice the smoke. A small, dense cloud of smoke was moving from the western ridge. Action was needed at once. Joe and Elaine had a small water tanker and with all the children aboard they crossed the paddocks to the western ridge as fast as the ancient tanker would take them. By this time the fire had extended to both the left- and right-hand sides of the slope and was moving slowly down the western ridge.

Elaine soon had the fire hose on the centre section of the fire, while Joe and the children, using wet bags, tried to contain the fire spreading rapidly to left and right. While the tanker and main hose were stopping the fire in the centre, the blaze was spreading out left and right and threatened to surround the cattle in the western paddock. The dry grass burnt easily and it was a tiring task. Fortunately the winds had dropped somewhat, otherwise the livestock would have been in a dangerous position.

Several hours went by and the heat and effort were wearing down both adults and children. To the left and right the fire soon reached an almost bare piece of ground. This was the break the fire fighters needed. With a last, strenuous effort, the centre section was extinguished and the left and right sections were brought under control.

Joe and Elaine were greatly relieved as the situation was now safe. Although very tired and blackened by the ash and smoke they stood and watched the last of the flames die out.

It had been an exciting day for Helen and Jason but they never before realised the difficulties faced by firefighters. Though exhausted, they were quite proud of their efforts and knew they had an interesting adventure to tell their parents on their return to the city.

ACTIVITY 1 Creating a narrative outline

Here is a basic outline for another narrative. Use questions based on the Five Ws—*who*, *when*, *where*, *why* and *what*—to extend it into a **final outline**. You can use the questions below or make up others yourself. (See page 1 if you need to revise the steps again.)

Karl, Karen — dog Rover — riding ranges — steep slope — snake frightened horses — riders crash down slope — injured — Karl hurt — tore part of shirt — dog's collar — home — long hot wait — blazing sun — suddenly sound of engine — parents — utility — rescue

- **Who** are the main characters?
- **What** are the main characters like?
- **What** are the horses like?
- **What** was the location of their favourite ride?
- **When** did they set out?
- **What** provisions did they take?
- **What** injuries did they receive?
- **Where** did Rover go?
- **How** did Karl manage to get the dog to run home?
- **What** were the weather conditions like?
- **When** did they hear the sound of rescue?

Final outline

Rover saves the day

ACTIVITY 2 Writing a narrative

Here is the first part of a narrative called *A strange encounter*.

Your tasks are to:

- **Read** the first part.
- **Brainstorm** and prepare a **final outline** for the remainder of the narrative on the lines below. (See page 2 if you need to revise this step again.)
- **Use** the **final outline** to **complete** the **first draft** of the remainder on a **separate** sheet of paper. (See page 3 if you need to revise this step again.)
- **Carry out Step 3**: Format and sequence checking. (See page 4 if you need to revise this step again.)
- **Carry out Step 4**: Reviewing and editing. (See page 4 if you need to revise this step again.)
- **Write** the final draft of the remainder of the narrative on the **next page**. (See page 6 if you need to revise this step again.)

A strange encounter

Late one Saturday afternoon Max, Sandra and Mike set off for the town of Tara. The dirt road was narrow in places and the town was forty-two kilometres from the homestead. As they continued on their way, the sun began to set slowly. Soon they had passed Dixon Creek and were heading up the slight hill beyond the bridge.

Suddenly, they were aware of a blue glow, which seemed to be coming from behind the hill. Puzzled by this strange glow, they stopped the car and crawled up the bank towards the top. As they came closer and closer to the summit, the glow became brighter. Reaching the top, their mouths wide in amazement, they saw …

Final outline

ACTIVITY 2 Writing a narrative

Final draft of remainder of narrative

Factual texts

A **recount** is a special type of report.

- It identifies a **series of events** and often makes a judgement of the value and importance of the events.
- The events in a recount are usually in **time order** and provide answers to questions based on the **Five Ws**: *Who*? *When*? *Where*? *What*? and *Why*?
- A recount is in **three sections**.

Orientation: who or what the recount is about
Events: when, where and why the event occurred
Evaluation: a judgement of the events

Task

Mark's task was to prepare a recount on two of Australia's early explorers: George Bass and Matthew Flinders.

Mark's first step was to **brainstorm** an **outline**. He listed a number of questions to help him with his basic outline.

- **Who** are the explorers?
- **When** did their journeys take place?
- **Where** did they travel?
- **Why** did they go exploring?
- **Which** vessels did they use?
- **Who** helped or encouraged them?

Mark then used **reference material** to answer the questions he had listed. His final outline is below.

Mark's final outline

- George Bass and Matthew Flinders — naval officers — arrived with Governor Hunter
- First journey 1795 — small rowing boat — called *Tom Thumb* — Sydney to the Georges River
- 1796 — other short trips
- 1797 — Bass given old whaling boat headed south — along Victorian coastline
- 1798 — Flinders given old sailing ship *Norfolk* — south from Sydney — down west coast of Tasmania — returned to Sydney
- 1801 — Flinders in the *Investigator* mapped the southern coast of Australia — from Western Australia — back to Sydney
- 1802 — Flinders — *Investigator* — sailed right around Australia
- Showed the way for new settlers — filled in many gaps in the map of Australia

Editing factual text

- **Read** the first draft Mark prepared.
- **Complete** a format and sequence check.
- **Review** and **edit** the recount.
- **Note** any changes you would make.

Mark's first draft

The journeys of Bass and Flinders

When Governor Hunter was sent to Sydney to run the colony, two naval officers accompanied him. George Bass and Matthew Flinders were both eager to explore the coastline of Australia and at first they made short expeditions together. because the colony was so poorly supplied, Hunter could only provide them with a small rowing boat each time. Both of the boats were called *Tom Thumb*.

In 1795, Bass and Flinders made their first trip they sailed from Sydney to the Georges River and then travelled up the river for a short distance.

In 1797, after other short trips, Bass was given an old whaling boat and a crew to row it. The crew rowed 2000 kilometres, heading south and then west along the Victorian coastline. Bass discovered Wilsons Promontory, Phillip Island and other islands in what is now called Bass Strait.

In 1798, Governor Hunter gave Flinders an old sailing ship, called the *Norfolk*. Flinders agreed with Bass that Van Diemen's Land (Tasmania) was most likely an island, and that the waters south of victoria were a strait, not a bay. Flinders travelled south from Sydny, turning west to follow the northern Tasmanian coast. He then travelled down the west coast, rounded the southern tip, and returned to Sydney. He named the strait after his friend Bass.

In 1802, Flinders circumnavigated Australia, starting north of Sydney. He travelled to Timor and then around Western Australia and back to Sydney.

In 1801, Flinders was ordered to sail from England to map the south coast of Australia in the *Investigator*. Arriving from the Indian Ocean, he sailed along the entire south coast, naming the Great Australian Bight before sailing around to Sydney.

Bass and Flinders maped much of the coast of Australia and showed the way for new settlers. Flinders was the first to suggest the name 'Australia' for the continent as a whole.

ACTIVITY 4 Writing a factual text (final outline)

Here is a basic list of questions to help you prepare a recount entitled *The amazing swimming career of Ian Thorpe*.

Brainstorming questions

- **Where** was he born?
- **Where** did he begin swimming?
- **What** were his earliest successes?
- **How** did he approach his training?
- **What** junior successes did he have?
- **When** did his career really begin to take off?
- **Which** major successes did he achieve in the Commonwealth Games and Olympic Games?
- **How** will Ian Thorpe be remembered?

Use **reference material** to complete the final outline.

Final outline

ACTIVITY 5 Writing a factual text (final draft)

- **Use** the **final outline** to complete the recount on a separate sheet of paper.
- **Carry out Step 3:** format and sequence checking.
- **Carry out Step 4:** reviewing and editing.
- **Complete** the **final draft** of the recount on the lines below.

Final draft

The amazing swimming career of Ian Thorpe

2 Making and using notes

In this chapter you will learn how to read and use **reference texts**. Using references effectively means **making notes** that you can use when you are preparing the outline for a **factual text**.

Making notes

- When you find a reference, the first step is to **decide** if it will **help** you to write your factual text.
- Note taking consists of **writing down information** in shortened form so that it can provide the basis for your work.

Rules for making notes

- **Read the whole section** before beginning to take notes.
- **Identify** and jot down **key words**. Most paragraphs have one main idea the author wants you to know.
- Next to the key words **write information** related to them in your own words.

Examples

Text: Captain Thunderbolt

One of Australia's most famous bushrangers, Captain Thunderbolt was born at Windsor in New South Wales in 1836. His real name was Frederick Ward, and as a young man he became a skilled horseman with a keen eye for a fast racehorse. His love of horses led him into trouble with the law, and he was arrested for horse stealing. Ward always claimed that he was innocent but it was to no avail and he was sentenced to a long prison term. Cockatoo Island in Sydney Harbour was a harsh prison from which it was said no one could escape. It was here that Ward was imprisoned.

Notes

famous — bushranger — Captain Thunderbolt — born Windsor — NSW — 1833 — real name Frederick Ward — skilled horseman. Horses — problem with law — arrested — stealing horses — declared himself innocent — sentenced — prison — Cockatoo Island — Sydney Harbour — harsh prison — difficult to escape.

Notes on Ludwig Leichhardt

Ludwig Leichhardt — Prussian — long journey — 1844–5 — Darling Downs to Port Essington — Northern Territory. Through Burdekin River valley — crossed Dividing Range — discovered Lynd and Mitchell Rivers — followed shores — Gulf Carpentaria — arrived Port Essington 1845.

Expanded notes

Ludwig Leichhardt was a Prussian explorer who completed a long journey during 1844–5 from the Darling Downs to Port Essington in the Northern Territory. His party travelled through the Burdekin River valley and crossed the Dividing Range. They discovered the Lynd and Mitchell Rivers. The party then followed the shores of the Gulf of Carpentaria. The expedition finally reached Port Essington in 1845.

ACTIVITY 1 Making notes

- **Read** the text below.
- **Look at** the table below. Notes for the first two key words have been completed for you.
- **Complete** notes for the remaining three key words.
- **Remember** that not **all** details are required.

The expeditions of Lord John Forrest

The journeys of John Forrest were in South Australia, Western Australia and the Northern Territory. He explored some of the harshest and most rugged country in Australia.

His **first expedition** was in 1869. He began his journey from Perth and went north-west to Lake Barlee, a round trip of approximately 1000 kilometres.

On his **second expedition**, begun in 1870, he again set out from Perth. Crossing over the south-western region of Western Australia he reached Esperance Bay. From there he travelled around the Great Australian Bight, crossing Eyre Peninsula and then travelling to Adelaide in South Australia. The route that he took was later used for the construction of the telegraph line linking Western Australia to the eastern states.

His **third expedition** was by far the most difficult. Forrest travelled with his brother Alexander and several Aboriginals. They set out from Geraldton and followed the Murchison River to its source in the Robinson Ranges. The group found it was **dangerous country** because water was very hard to find. The Aboriginals were very useful as one of them, Tommy Windich, had a particular skill at finding water. Often supplies were very low. They did, however, find two significant springs, which were named Weld and Windich Springs.

Much of the land they travelled through was a sand and rock wasteland, with spinifex being the common plant. For weeks they travelled eastwards, suffering in the terrible heat where many lakes were salt lakes. Eventually they reached the Overland Telegraph Line at Peake Station in South Australia. From there the expedition travelled south to Adelaide.

This was a remarkable expedition as it crossed some of the most desolate areas of Australia. As a **result** the government now knew that much of this country was quite unsuitable for European settlement.

Notes on John Forrest

Key words	Notes
first expedition	1869 — Perth — NW — Lake Barlee — 1000 kilometres round trip
second expedition	1870 — Perth — Esperance Bay — across Great Australian Bight — Eyre Peninsula — Adelaide
third expedition	
dangerous country	
result	

ACTIVITY 2 Using notes

- **Read** the section below. It is the first part of a writing task: *Write a report on the journeys of John Forrest*.
- **See** how the notes have been extended into sentences.
- **Notice** that the information is the same but is written differently. In other words, the writer has not copied the original but used her own words.
- **Complete** the report, expanding the notes you prepared for the last three key words.

Report on the journeys of John Forrest

John Forrest set out on his first journey in 1869. From Perth he travelled north-west to Lake Barlee, a distance of about 1000 kilometres.

On his second journey he used Perth as his starting point. He crossed the country to Esperance Bay and then across the Great Australian Bight. After travelling over Eyre Peninsula, he finally reached Adelaide.

ACTIVITY 3 Making notes

- **Read** the extract below.
- **Notes** for the first key word have been completed for you.
- **Your task** is to complete notes for the remaining four key words.
- **Remember** that not all details are required.

The English longbow

Bows and arrows have been used for thousands of years for battle and hunting.

Early bows were often made from layers of animal horn and sinew. Often these were small bows and they were very useful for mounted warriors because of their compact size.

The **English longbow** was made from one long piece of wood. While many types of wood were used, yew was considered the best for making a longbow. The bow was about 1.8 metres long and tapered from the centre towards each end. Notches at the ends held the loop of string.

The English realised the **value of the longbow** during the Welsh Wars of the twelfth century. By the thirteenth century there were large numbers of bowmen in the English armies. English successes at the battles of Crecy in 1346, Poitiers in 1356 and Agincourt in 1415 were due to the power of the longbow.

English bowmen required some special **skills** to use the longbow effectively. It required strength and much practice to use it correctly. It was best to be able to string the arrow, pull back, aim it and release the arrow all in one smooth and swift movement.

Using the longbow meant holding the string by the first three fingers of the right hand. A leather guard was used to protect the fingers and a bracer was worn on the arm to prevent the string from grazing the arm. An experienced bowman could get off up to twelve arrows in one minute.

The English longbow was a powerful weapon of war until the sixteenth century.

Notes on the longbow

Key words	Notes
early bows	Made from animal horn — sinew — useful — mounted warriors — compact size
English longbow	
value of the longbow	
skills	
using the longbow	

ACTIVITY 4 Using notes

- **Use** the **notes** on the longbow to write a report entitled *The longbow in history*.
- **Remember** that the information will be the same but the original must not be copied. You must complete the report **in your own words**.

Your report

The longbow in history

ACTIVITY 5 Making notes

This activity gives you practice **locating suitable key words** in order to make notes.

- **Read** the report below on *Bears of the world*.
- **Check** if the article is in **sections** so that main ideas can be identified easily.
- **List** the **key words**.
- **Complete** the **notes** for each key word.

Bears of the world

Bears are found in many countries but mostly in the northern hemisphere. They are strongly built animals with thick coats. Their feet are flat and wide. Their claws are strong and quite long. Bears have good hearing and a very developed sense of smell.

Brown bears are found in Europe, Asia and North America. The two brown bears of North America are the Grizzly and the Kodiak bears. The Kodiak bear is the largest of all bears. It can stand 2.8 metres high and weigh over 700 kilograms.

Black bears include the Himalayan black bear and the Sun bear. The Himalayan black bear stands about 1.5 metres high and weighs over 100 kilograms. It lives in Asia, in the mountainous region sometimes up to 4000 metres above sea level.

Polar bears live in the Arctic region. Because of their creamy-white colour they are difficult to see on the ice and snow. Polar bears are expert swimmers and divers. They have been sighted swimming up to 65 kilometres from land.

Food sources for bears consist of both plant and animal food. Bears are particularly fond of insects, fruit and wild honey. Some bears also eat meat and fish as well. Because they often eat both types of food they are regarded as 'omnivorous' feeders.

Notes on bears of the world

Key words	Notes

ACTIVITY 6 Making notes

This gives you more practice **locating suitable key words** in order to make notes.

- **Read** the report below.
- **Identify** the sections so that the key words can be listed.
- **Write** the key words.
- **Complete** the notes for each key word.

Karakamia Sanctuary (pronounced Karak-a-mia)

The Australian Wildlife Conservation (AWC) is an organisation that has as its main aim the conservation of Australian wildlife. The AWC began its work in 1991 when the founder, Martin Copley, set up the Karakamia Sanctuary in Western Australia. The organisation now owns twelve properties across Australia. These cover almost 600 000 hectares. These sanctuaries provide for the protection of many different ecosystems and a wide variety of plant and animal life.

Australian Wildlife Conservation sets up these sanctuaries where controls on feral animals and weeds are in place, and threatened animals are then reintroduced.

Australia has a high rate of extinction of animals, with over twenty animals now extinct and more than fifty listed as endangered. The greatest threats to our native wildlife are foxes and feral cats. Our native wildlife also faces other dangers, namely competition with feral animals such as goats and rabbits.

The Karakamia Sanctuary is located in a jarrah forest east of Perth. It was set up with the building of nine kilometres of vermin-proof fencing around the 260 hectares. Foxes and feral cats are excluded by this fence. Several species of animals have been reintroduced. These include the woylie, numbat, quenda, Tamar wallaby, quokka and Western Ringtail possum.

The sanctuary is a shining example of what can be done to avoid the further extinction of Australian native birds and animals. Karakamia is home to 100 different types of birds, twenty-four types of reptiles and nine frog species. To visit the sanctuary at night and observe the many native animals on the ground and in the trees is an exciting experience.

Notes on Karakamia Sanctuary

Key words	Notes

Making notes

- **Read** the biography below.
- **Identify** the sections so that the key words can be listed.
- **Write** the key words.
- **Complete** the notes for each key word.
- Then complete the activity by **writing your report** in your own words.

'Banjo' Paterson

One of Australia's greatest poets, Andrew Barton Paterson was born in 1864. The eldest of seven children, he grew up on stations near Orange in New South Wales.

When he was ten years old he was sent to Sydney to attend Sydney Grammar School. While there he lived with his grandmother at Illawong. After completing his schooling he became an articled clerk in a solicitor's office. He qualified as a solicitor himself in 1886 and worked with John William Street for several years.

He began writing poetry for the *Bulletin* magazine under the name 'Banjo'. Over a period of ten years he wrote some very popular poetry. Such poems as 'Clancy of the Overflow', 'The Man from Ironbark' and 'The Man from Snowy River' made him one of Australia's favourite writers. As a celebrity, Paterson travelled the country, writing verses and stories about his experiences. In 1899 he became a war correspondent in the Boer War. He also reported on the Boxer rebellion in China and the Great War of 1914–1918.

After the end of the Great War, Paterson and his family lived in Sydney. He continued to write and he published several children's books. He also became a broadcaster for the ABC. In 1939 he received an award for his service to Australian literature. Two years later this great Australian storyteller died, leaving his wife and two children.

Paterson's verse had great appeal. It combined exciting yarns, comic situations and incidents where courage, mateship and love of country were very evident. His work is still popular today.

Notes on 'Banjo' Paterson

Key words	Notes

Your report

Biography of 'Banjo' Paterson

ACTIVITY 9 Using notes

One of the most exciting series of films in recent times is The Lord of the Rings trilogy. The first film in the series was *The Fellowship of the Ring*.

- **View** the first part of the film.
- **Use** the notes below to prepare an introduction to the film.

Story — Middle Earth — many years ago
Back in mists of time — great rings forged
Three to elves, seven to dwarf lords, nine to men
Rings — strength — will govern wisely
One other ring forged — at Mordor — Mt Doom
Saron — master ring — rule all Middle Earth
Mordor — vanquished — many free lands fell
Alliance — men, elves — great battle — Saron defeated
Ring taken — son of King — King lost master ring
New wearer — Gollom
Gollom — lived many years — ring left Gollom
Picked up — Bilbo Baggins of the Shire — master ring

Introduction

3 Examining a topic

In this chapter you will learn how to respond to five of the most common **instructional verbs**. Instructional verbs are used to tell you how a writing project is to be completed.

Describe	To describe is to provide an imaginatively written description of an object, event or situation. It should appeal to the senses of sight, sound, smell, taste and touch.
Discuss	To discuss is to provide a complete and detailed response to a topic, which may include an incident or event. The important points should be emphasised and the positive and negative points of view should be included.
Narrate	To narrate means to tell a story or provide an account of an event or particular experience. A writer may narrate a series of events in his or her life. These may be factual or imaginary. *Narrate* can also be used for reports.
Compare	To compare two items, incidents or situations you should look for those aspects, qualities or characteristics that are similar. While some of the main differences may be mentioned, the emphasis should be on similarities.
Summarise	To summarise is to look over a topic and provide only the main points. Minor details are not required and lengthy explanations should be avoided.

During high school and beyond you will encounter many other instructional verbs used for assignment writing, but these are the main ones.

Describe

To **describe** is to provide a **'word picture'** of the subject of the writing project. The description should include the main parts, workings, shapes, colours, dimensions, sounds and feelings. Careful choice of words will make a description come to life.

Example

Describe the last few hours of the wreck of the *Ellendale*.

The key words are *describe* and *last few hours*. The description should clearly show how the sailing ship *Ellendale* was finally swamped.

The wind was increasing rapidly. From a gentle breeze it had turned into a howling gale. The sea rose and fell much more quickly. Across the stretch of water, as far as the eye could see, tall, white foam caps appeared on the threatening waves. Soon the sailing craft *Ellendale* was surrounded by long, heaving waves crashing into her sides. The sound of each massive breaker warned of extreme danger.

The small sailing craft *Ellendale* was now in distress. The roaring, shrieking winds had been attacking her all night long. The dull, sickly dawn revealed her canvas torn to shreds and the ropes and rigging in complete disarray.

The tall masts trembled and the ship's timbers were straining as each boiling surge of water crashed around her.

The ship's last hours were at hand. The huge dark green, foam-capped waves rose in front and washed down onto her damaged decking. For two hours the ship was in violent combat with the elements.

Soon the weary sailors stared in horror, as on the port bow a huge rogue wave rolled towards the stricken craft. The vessel lurched. The massive wave gathered momentum and lifted her sideways. Two weakened masts split and tumbled to the deck. Listing heavily, the now doomed craft slid towards the rushing turmoil of water in a deep trough. Suddenly it was all over as a cascade of foam and water washed onto the vessel and it lay helplessly on its side. Within a few minutes it had slid into the deep and disappeared forever.

ACTIVITY 1 Describing a topic

Use the notes below to **write** a **description** of about twenty lines. Use your own words. Your topic is:

Describe the life cycle of the Alaskan salmon.

Early years — cold fresh water — mountain streams
Leave creeks and rivers — head — deep waters — Pacific Ocean grow further
Fully grown — begin great migration
Reach coast — travel up — reach — area where hatched
Predators — bears — birds — at work
Overcome — waterfalls — rapids — powerful leaps
Reach spawning ground — eggs laid — salmon die
New generation — ready — amazing life cycle

Discuss

To **discuss** a topic you should provide a complete and **detailed answer**. You should examine the subject closely by writing in detail, emphasising the important points and mentioning both positive and negative points of view if they apply.

Example

Discuss the importance of the development of the early railways in England.

The key words are *discuss* and *importance*. The detail of how the railways came about is necessary but the importance of the rail system must be stressed.

Simple forms of railways were in use in England in the seventeenth century. Horses drew wagons along wooden rails. Iron rails came into use in the eighteenth century.

While many canals had been built and barges were used to carry all types of goods, an engine was needed for hauling wagonloads of coal and other commodities.

The first railway locomotive was built by Richard Trevithick, a Cornish inventor. An engine of his design ran from Darlington to Stockton, a distance of twenty kilometres, in September 1825.

George Stephenson further developed an engine to haul coal wagons on the Stockton–Darlington railway. He was the first engineer to build a locomotive engine, which could haul three times its own weight at over twenty-four kilometres per hour. The engine was called the *Rocket* and it led to the opening of the Liverpool and Manchester railways.

Large amounts of money were invested in railways. Railway trains could carry goods and passengers more quickly than wagons or canal boats. In the north-east of England canals were quite rare. The development of railway systems meant that the carriage of heavy articles was speeded up and freight costs were reduced.

Soon there was a network of railway lines across England. The early railways were important because they meant transport, for both people and goods, was easier and more reliable. Further improvements were made to the railways, and railway engines and railway technology were exported to almost every continent. This enabled new areas of mining and production to be developed in many parts of the world.

ACTIVITY 2 Writing a discussion

Use the notes below to **write**, in your own words, a **discussion** approximately twenty lines long. Your topic is:

Discuss the early training of the great artist Michelangelo.

Born 6 March 1475 — Caprese — Italy.
Sent by parents to Settignano — stayed with family stonemasons.
There learnt use hammer and chisel.
Brought back to Florence — apprenticed — painter — Ghirlandaio studio.
Developed painting skills — really wanted — sculptor.
Selected — join — Medici school.
Michelangelo lived — Medici palace — more painting and drawing lessons.
Teacher Bertoldo — worked students hard.
Began working in clay — then used sculptors' tools — created first sculpture.
Training — helped — skills — became great painter — sculptor.

Narrate

To **narrate** means to provide a **narrative** or **story**. The narrative may be of a factual event or an imaginary account.

Examples

- Narrate the steps taken in converting bauxite to aluminium. (factual)
- Narrate the events prior to a family trip overseas. (factual or imaginary)

In both examples the key word is *narrate*. In the first example the actual **steps taken** make up the narrative. In the second all the **events that took place before** the actual trip are narrated. A narrative for the second example is given below.

The first step we took was to discuss our holiday plan with a travel agent. It was our intention to travel to Noumea in New Caledonia for a week and then fly across to Isle of Pines for another few days. Our travel agent attended to all the details and provided us with a schedule of flights and accommodation details.

We then checked that our passports were up to date for travel.

Steve, our big brother, bought a guide book. Because French is the main language, a small book of useful phrases was also purchased.

It was important that we knew which items we were allowed to carry on board. We found this information on the AQIS website.

Close to departure date, we all packed our clothes and personal effects in the bags we had selected for the trip.

Our parents then arranged for us to be taken to the airport by our best friends.

Now all we had to do was enjoy the flight and a holiday in the South Pacific.

ACTIVITY 3 Writing a narrative

Use the notes below to **write** in your own words a **narrative** of approximately twenty lines. Your topic is:

Narrate the history of the development of the Australian horse, the Waler.

No horses — Australia — before European settlement.
Seven horses — first fleet — only two survived few years.
Imported — mares — South Africa — stallions and mares — England.
Other horses — Dutch — Spanish — English thoroughbreds — Arabian.
Gradually distinctive Australian horse — Waler.
Waler — became strong horse — great stamina — good jumper.
Other imports — good breeding — better stock — Waler — reputation — courage, strength, endurance.
Many Walers — overseas — World War I — Australian cavalry horses.
Not allowed return Australia.
Reduced numbers — breed declined — no longer recorded — stud book.

Compare

To **compare** two items, incidents or situations you have to look for the aspects of the subjects that are **similar**.

Example

Compare the effects of the growth of the wool industry and the gold rush on the development of Australia.

The key words are *compare* and *effects*. Compare means 'look closely at those aspects that are similar'. There is nothing wrong with mentioning some of the differences, but only the similarities should be explained in detail.

Wool and gold have had a great influence on the development of Australia. From the early 1800s onwards the wool industry helped increase the population as new settlers arrived to take up grazing lands. The wool industry increased the wealth of individuals and districts.

Gold brought prosperity first to New South Wales and Victoria. The first gold discovery was at Summerhill Creek near Bathurst in 1851. This was followed by finds at Ballarat and Bendigo. Queensland was next to benefit from a large discovery, at Gympie in 1867.

Gold mining also resulted in increased population and wealth but at a much faster rate. Prospectors from many lands rushed to try their luck on the gold fields.

The discovery of gold in Australia meant that the states became rich enough to build roads and railways to further develop the country. Gold was the first great stepping stone in Australia's progress.

Wool also made a great contribution to Australia's wealth. It became the greatest export product and Australia was the world's chief wool producer. The growth of the wool industry led to a great increase in workers in country areas, from pastoralists, shearers and transport workers to scientists.

Wool production and gold mining both led to the development of regional towns and improvements to transport. Both brought money into the states. Cities grew larger and factories were built to cater for the larger population and the needs of the graziers and mining community.

The expansion of settlements brought about by wool and gold allowed for great progress in transport and communications, banking, industries and exports.

ACTIVITY 4 Writing a comparison

Use the notes below to **write**, in your own words, a **comparison** of approximately twenty lines. Your topic is:

Compare the size, surface and structure of the two planets Jupiter and Venus.

Jupiter — largest planet — 1000 times larger than Earth.
Venus — much smaller — about same size — Earth.
Jupiter — atmosphere — mainly hydrogen, helium.
Venus — atmosphere — mainly carbon dioxide — some nitrogen — sulphur dioxide.
Jupiter — below huge dense clouds — composed of solid hydrogen — has electric currents through it.
Venus — small hot planet — surface temperature — melt lead.
Venus — high thick clouds — rocky surface — similar to Earth — waterless surface.
Jupiter — frozen giant — Venus — small inferno.

ACTIVITY 5 Writing a comparison

Two commemorative days significant for Australian history are Anzac Day and Remembrance Day. Both these annual observances have been part of Australian culture for many years.

1. Use the Internet to complete this activity. **Read** these **websites**:
   - http://www.acn.net.au/articles/anzac/
   - http://www.dva.gov.au/commem/rememb/rem_origin.htm
2. Use the information to **write** in your own words a **comparison** of approximately 20 lines. Your topic is:

Compare these two days in terms of the following:

- reasons for establishment of these days as 'special' days
- the countries that regard these as special days
- the types of ceremonies conducted and a brief description of them.

Summarise

To **summarise** it is necessary to look over a topic and then **present** the **main points**. Minor details can be omitted, along with lengthy explanations.

Example

Summarise the ways households can help save water supplies.

Each household has a duty to minimise the waste of our precious resource—water.

A first step in helping save water is to ensure that all taps and other water fittings do not leak.

The fitting of water saving taps and shower devices should be considered. Toilet cisterns that use a smaller volume of water could also be installed.

The installation of rainwater tanks will mean that an additional supply of water is on hand.

Outdoor areas, lawn and gardens can be watered with grey water (water from showers, baths and washing machines), as well as tank water.

Avoiding frequent use of dishwasher and washing machine will help save water.

For individuals it is important to reduce time in the shower and use a small volume of water if using a bath.

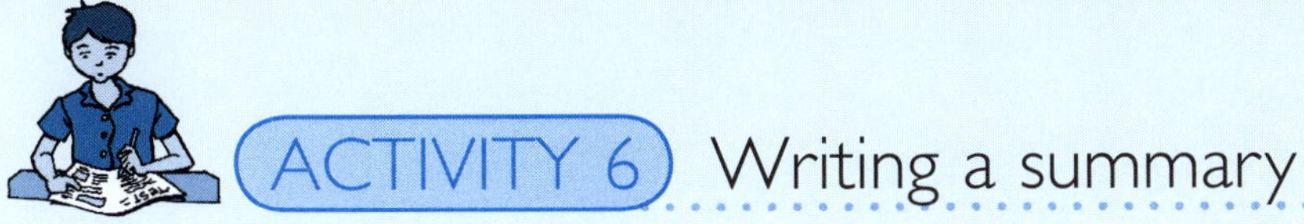

ACTIVITY 6 Writing a summary

Use the notes below to **write**, in your own words, a 10–15 line **summary**. Your topic is:

Summarise the short history of the clipper ships.

Clippers — large well built — great sail area.
Value — very fast — last great sailing ships.
First clipper — *Ann McKim* — built 1832 — Baltimore USA.
Clippers — fast trading ships — many types of goods — passengers as well — also slave trade.
Carried goods — people — across oceans — record *Andrew Jackson* — 1852 — England to New York — 15 days.
Lightning — England to Australia — up to 700 kilometres per day.
After 1870 — use declined — steamships more profitable.

ACTIVITY 7 Writing a summary

One of the most entertaining series of books and films of recent times has been the Harry Potter series. The first book and film in the series was *Harry Potter and the Philosopher's Stone*. It contained many amusing and exciting incidents.

Select one of the incidents from the box and **write** a **summary** of the incident in **five** or **six sentences**. (You may then choose a second incident and write a summary of it, if you like.)

Your **summary** should include **three sections**:

- characters
- setting
- description of incident.

Incidents

- The letters for Harry arriving at the house on Privet Drive
- The appearance of the huge bearded man, the Keeper of the Keys, at the coastal cottage on Harry's eleventh birthday
- The process used by the Hogwarts school to divide the new students into four houses

4 Punctuation and writing conventions

In this chapter you will learn to use **proper punctuation** so that you can build sentences that will make your **meaning clear**.

Read this short **unpunctuated** paragraph.

as quietly as he could james moved towards the shed there was a creature hidden there what could it be whatever it was it should not have been there fixing his gaze on a small shrub nearby he crept even closer a low growl could be heard james did not move hadn't his father told him the stories of the highland wild cats it must be one of them he murmured quietly to himself

Now **read** this correctly **punctuated** paragraph.

As quietly as he could James moved towards the shed. There was a creature hidden there. What could it be? Whatever it was it should not have been there. Fixing his gaze on a small shrub nearby he crept even closer. A low growl could be heard. James did not move. Hadn't his father told him the stories of the highland wild cats?

'It must be one of them', he murmured quietly to himself.

Making your meaning clear

The two sentences below have exactly the **same words** but **different meanings** because they are punctuated differently.

Example

The owner said, 'Paula will attend to the task'.

'The owner', said Paula, 'will attend to the task'.

Punctuation conventions

The punctuation and writing conventions necessary for written material are:

- capitals and full stops
- commas, question marks, exclamation marks
- apostrophes, colons, semicolons
- hyphens, dashes, brackets
- numbers, measurements, dates, times
- abbreviations, contractions, acronyms
- direct and indirect speech.

Correct punctuation is as important when writing as correct grammatical structure.

Capitals and full stops

Capitals

Capitals are used for:

- the **first word** in a **sentence**
- **proper names**
  - the names of people, places and pets
  - the names of books, plays and poems
  - the names of nationalities, battles and wars
  - the names of countries, states, cities, towns and streets
  - the names of mountains, rivers and oceans.

Examples

- **S**he did not know that he was away.
- **L**isa and **R**ae have gone to the theatre.
- All the students visited **G**rey **P**ark last week.
- My cat, **S**imba, is over twenty years old.
- The book ***K**idnapped* is a great novel.
- Have you read the play ***M**uch **A**do about **N**othing*?
- The poem '**T**he **M**an from **S**nowy **R**iver' is my favourite.
- Have you met our **J**apanese neighbour?
- The **B**attle of **H**astings took place in 1066.
- The **H**undred **Y**ears **W**ar lasted for a long time.
- The tourist visited **C**anada last month.
- There have been a number of severe bushfires in **V**ictoria.
- The federal capital of **A**ustralia is **C**anberra.
- The town of **W**arra is almost out of water.
- The girl lived in **V**anessa **S**treet.
- Have you ever been to the **B**lue **M**ountains?
- The **A**mazon **R**iver is in **S**outh **A**merica.
- She sailed across the **P**acific **O**cean in her yacht.

Capitals are also used for:

- **I**, I've, I'd, I'm
- **titles**, initials and university degrees
- **names** of homes, homesteads, stations, businesses and companies.

Examples

- **I**'ve often travelled to that Pacific island.
- **D**r **E**llen **M**athers lived in that apartment.
- The lecturer was Steven Ellis **BS**c, **MA**.
- Their home, **L**akeview, was on the edge of Lake Barrine.
- The cattle property **E**langa covered ten thousand hectares.
- The business **A**lana **P**ty **L**td completed the construction.

Full stops

Full stops are used for:

- the **end** of a **sentence**
- some **abbreviations**.

Examples

- She had visited the house lately**.**
- av**.** (= average), esp**.** (= especially), max**.** (= maximum)

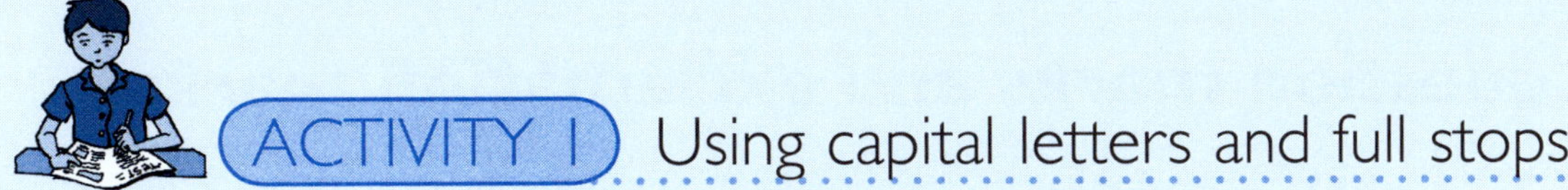

ACTIVITY 1 Using capital letters and full stops

1 **Identify** the words that need **capital letters**. **Mark** them in red.

a jack, michella and andy had been to Melbourne last july.

b on tuesday brad and tina went by rail to the Gippsland region to visit the neilson family.

c during the month of april the reverend g l ashton bought a new ford sedan.

d the family had moved from altandi street in the suburb of sunnybank to clarkson road in Macgregor.

e the ellison expedition travelled along the wanaka river until it reached toronto gulf.

f the jenolan caves in the blue mountains just west of sydney have become a great tourist attraction.

2 **Identify** the words that need **capital letters**. **Mark** them in red. **Insert full stops** where required. (There are three sentences in each part.)

a mt everest is one of the group of three peaks standing astride the tibet–nepal frontier a high level valley leads to the three giants—everest, lhotse and nuptse the valley itself slopes from about 5000 to 6000 metres high in a westerly direction

b roald amundsen was born near oslo, in norway, on 16 july 1872 as a boy he was fascinated by the travels of sir john franklin and his search for the north-west passage by 1897 he was appointed first mate of the belgica to travel to antarctica

c after the battle of zama the second punic war ended at the end of the day there were 20 000 troops on the field and the romans captured an additional 20 000 the power of the carthaginian empire collapsed with the defeat of hannibal

3 **Insert** words with **capital letters** in the spaces in these sentences.

a I think ____________ saw the ____________ lighthouse on the coast of ____________.

b The sheep station ____________ is situated several kilometres from ____________.

c The removal business ____________ took care when moving their furniture from their old home in ____________ to their new home in ____________.

d Has ____________ sailed across ____________ to Tasmania?

e ____________ and ____________ went to the theatre at ____________ to view the play ____________.

Commas, question marks and exclamation marks

Commas

Commas **separate persons** or **items**.

Examples

- Sam**,** Tien**,** Elle and Marion went to the show.
- They collected the knives**,** forks**,** spoons and plates.
- All the gold**,** silver**,** tin and lead were separated.

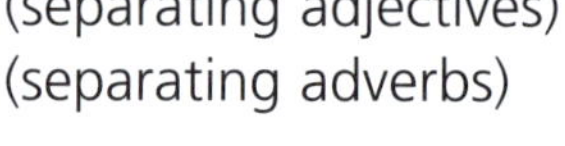

Note: there is no comma before *and* for the last person or item.

Commas **separate adjectives** and **adverbs**.

Examples

- She was a young**,** cheerful**,** enthusiastic worker. (separating adjectives)
- Slowly**,** carefully and quietly they completed the work. (separating adverbs)

Commas **separate phrases** and **clauses**.

Examples

- Jason worked on the painting in the morning**,** in the evening and at the weekend. (separating phrases)
- Though he was sick**,** he completed the work**,** but it was not to his usual high standard. (separating clauses)

Commas **separate introductory** or **single** words.

Examples

- Instead**,** they remained in the cave all week.
- His young cousin**,** Carolyn**,** played on the beach.

Question marks

Question marks are used at the **end** of a **question**.

Examples

- 'Why are you late**?**' she asked.
- How is it possible for this to be repaired**?**

Exclamation marks

Exclamation marks are used at the **end** of an **exclamation**, sentence or phrase that needs to be **emphasised**.

Examples

- 'What a goal**!**' he exclaimed.
- 'Take a good look at this work**!**' the supervisor shouted.
- How stupid**!**
- Be careful**!**

ACTIVITY 2 Using commas, question marks and exclamation marks

1. **Insert commas** where required in these sentences.
   - a Many of the old broken yellow desks were badly damaged.
   - b Some of the young frisky brown ponies galloped across the fields.
   - c Pelicans ducks and swans were on the clear blue lake.
   - d Alan Marco Guiseppe Alex and Sven all travelled to the show in the town.
   - e My cousins lived in Atherton Mt Garnet Cairns Cooktown and Innisfail.
   - f At three o'clock six o'clock nine o'clock and midnight the bells were rung.

2. **Check** the **commas** in these sentences. If they are correct, put a **tick** (✓) in the box. If not, put a **cross** (✗) in the box and **insert** commas in the correct places.
   - a The girl, who had collected the present, returned home immediately. ☐
   - b The soldiers, attacked quickly quietly and mercilessly. ☐
   - c My eldest, brother Adam has been there before. ☐
   - d Briony was a happy, smiling, hard working employee. ☐
   - e Fortunately, the small parcel, which we thought was lost, turned up later. ☐

3. **Read** the sentences. If the sentence requires an exclamation mark, **write E** in the box. If it requires a question mark, **write Q**.
   - a What a racket ☐
   - b Where is the racquet I gave you ☐
   - c Do it now ☐
   - d When are you going to the movies ☐
   - e Look out Bricks are falling ☐

4. **Insert exclamation** and **question marks** where required in these sentences.
   - a Help me, I'm slipping
   - b Ouch that really hurts
   - c 'Why are you here ' he asked
   - d Where are your books
   - e What a mess
   - f How do you repair the machine

Apostrophes, colons and semicolons

Apostrophes

Apostrophes are used in **abbreviated** words. The apostrophe stands for the **missing letters**.

Examples

- did not ➡ didn**'**t
- should not ➡ shouldn**'**t
- she will ➡ she**'**ll
- I am ➡ I**'**m
- who is ➡ who**'**s

Apostrophes are also used to indicate **ownership** or possession.

Add **apostrophe + *s*** for **singular words** owning items.

Examples

- girl**'s** dress
- cat**'s** tail
- horse**'s** mane

Add an **apostrophe** after the ***s*** in **plural words** that end in ***s***, ***es*** or ***ies***.

Examples

- boys**'** bicycles
- foxes**'** tails
- ladies**'** umbrellas

Add **apostrophe + *s*** for **plural words** that do not end in ***s***.

Examples

- women**'s** handbags
- men**'s** shirts
- children**'s** clothes

Colons

Colons are used to **introduce lists**. The colon is not followed by a capital letter and is rarely used.

Examples

- The team enjoyed a variety of sports**:** riding, football, tennis, swimming, archery and volleyball.
- The truck transported the following items**:** steel piping, concrete tanks, drums of fuel, bales of wool, building blocks and sawn timber.

Semicolons

Semicolons are used to **separate parts** of a **longer sentence** that are closely linked. Each part will make sense on its own. Like colons, semicolons are rarely used.

Examples

- The adult chose the weapon**;** it was a sharp, broad sword.
- The sound of the crackling twig gave me a terrible fright**;** I was totally afraid.

ACTIVITY 3 Using apostrophes, colons and semicolons

1 **Rewrite** using **apostrophes**.

Examples: could not = couldn't cars of the men = men's cars

a cannot ______

b has not ______

c over ______

d of the clock ______

e they would ______

f who have ______

g it is ______

h you will ______

i the cry of a baby ______

j the coats of the women ______

k the tails of the tigers ______

l the hats of the gentlemen ______

2 **Add apostrophes** as required.

a these farmers crops
b the mans wife
c several teachers classes
d these birds nests

3 **Identify** the words that require **apostrophes**. Mark them.

a The ladies purses were left on shelves.
b My friends car is by that girls home.
c These monkeys tails are longer than that horses tail.
d The fishermens nets lay on the strangers boat.
e The acrobats skill entertained the crowd in the towns showground.
f His friends rifle was next to his cousins spear gun.

4 **Add** a **colon** in the correct position in these sentences.

a The plumber carried many items spanners, pairs of pliers, drills, shovels, pipes, plastic sheeting and containers.
b These containers were used to hold many substances oil, water, mower fuel, detergent, solvent and waste water.

5 **Add** a **semicolon** in the correct position in these sentences.

a She collected the basket it was really well made.
b The silence was broken by a ticking sound my heart missed a beat.

Hyphens, dashes and brackets

Hyphens

Hyphens are used to **unite two** or **more words** that spend most of their time apart from one another.

Examples

- son-in-law
- vice-president
- semi-annual
- two-storey home
- one-quarter

Hyphens are also used to **avoid confusion** by keeping two or more parts of a compound word apart.

Examples

- driftice ➡ drift-ice
- culdesac ➡ cul-de-sac
- reinvent ➡ re-invent

Dashes

Dashes are used to **separate** a **comment** of **less importance**.

Example

The rain fell so heavily for several days—two and one half actually—that it was impossible to leave home.

Brackets

Brackets are used **around details** that, while **not absolutely necessary**, add to the understanding of the text.

Examples

- Mt Everest **(**in the Himalayas**)** is the world's highest mountain.
- This comprehensive reference book **(**of five hundred and twenty pages**)** is the most useful book on geology that I own.
- That veteran player **(**over three hundred first grade games**)** was one of the most durable five-eighths in the game.

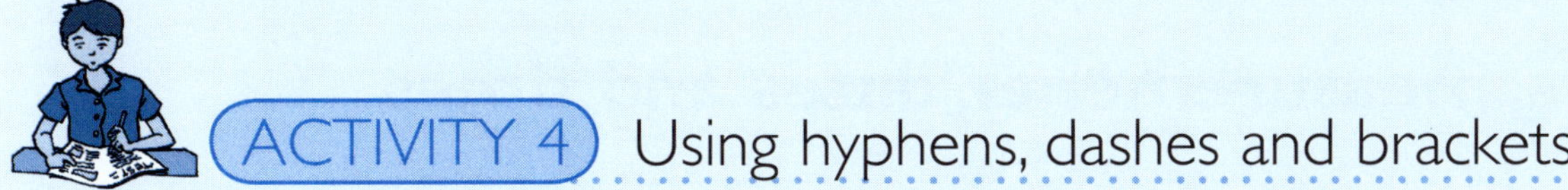

ACTIVITY 4 Using hyphens, dashes and brackets

1 **Write** the words below correctly, **inserting hyphens** as required.

a pitapat ____________________

b stickinthemud ____________________

c ninetenths ____________________

d antiwar ____________________

e sealegs ____________________

f roundup ____________________

g birdtable ____________________

h clearcut ____________________

i ninetynine ____________________

j stakeout ____________________

2 **Circle** the words that require hyphens in these sentences. **Write** them correctly in the spaces.

a They used jetblack paint to cover the damaged section.

____

b All the students were in a lighthearted mood after the tests were completed.

____

c The horse and rider were wellprepared for the special dressage event.

____

d Many of the coordinators of the display had worked for many days.

____

e The antiwhaling discussions did not really make any difference to the situation.

____

3 **Identify** where **dashes** could be placed in these sentences. **Insert** them.

a The journey was particularly long fifteen months to be exact and required great stamina.

b It was a day of blazing heat temperature as high as 35°C so that everyone suffered greatly.

c Mary was very gifted in artistic skills pottery, painting, sculpture, collage work and screen printing.

d There they stood on the top of the mountain kilometres from any civilisation and enjoyed the solitude.

4 **Insert brackets** where necessary in the following sentences.

a That progressive company founded in the USA has been expanding in Australia for decades.

b The talented youngster already a winner in the singles teamed with his brother in the doubles.

c Many of the books more than one hundred of them that I have read are in the local library.

d The instructions for use see page 36 of the manual have been written in simple English.

Numbers, measurements, dates and times

Numbers

In most writing, numbers **below 100** are expressed in **words**. Numbers **above** and **including 100** are usually expressed in **numerical form**.

Examples thirty-seven 297

Approximate numbers are usually expressed in **words**.

Example There were approximately seven thousand troops on the field.

Spaces are normally used in numbers of **five** or **more digits**.

Examples 3721 37 217 3 721 731

Small amounts of **money** are usually expressed in **words**, but **larger amounts** are usually expressed in **numerals**.

Examples two dollars and fifty cents $38.75 $129.75 $6702.40

Approximate amounts are usually expressed in **words**.

Example The cost of the building was in excess of four million dollars.

Measurements

In **general texts** measurements are usually in **words** (unless the numbers are too long when written out).

Examples

- There were eighty kilograms of lead in the box.
- The property covered thirty hectares.

In **scientific** or **technical texts**, where precise amounts are dealt with, **numerals** and abbreviated units of measurement are used.

Examples

- The length of the expanded tube was 39.38 cm.
- All of the containers held 34.23 g.

Dates and times

Dates should be written using the following forms.

Examples

15 August 2007 Wednesday, 15 August 2007
15.08.07 15.08.2007

Time should be expressed in **words**.

Examples

- Sharon usually woke at seven o'clock.
- Jack travelled on the nine-twenty bus to town.

In **scientific** or **technical texts** time is usually expressed in the following forms.

Examples 7.25 p.m. 6.20 a.m.

ACTIVITY 5 Using numbers, measurements, dates and times

1. **Identify** the **number** or **money amount**. **Underline** it. If the correct form is used in the sentence, **tick** (✓) the box. If the correct form is not used, **mark** a **cross** (✗) in the box and **write** it correctly.
   - a He found that there were 49 pencils in the box. ☐ ______
   - b Jane had found 460 beads to use on her craft work. ☐ ______
   - c Tien decided to save the three dollars eighty cents she had been given. ☐ ______
   - d The business was sold last year for over $600 000. ☐ ______
   - e Do you think that that coat is actually worth $160? ☐ ______
   - f The credit card bill showed that he owed no less than $3975.15. ☐ ______

2. **Circle** the **measurements** in these sentences. **Write** them in correct form.
   - a Theo found that the height of the building was 4 metres.

     ______

     ______
   - b The science teacher explained that the brass rod had expanded by three thousandths of a millimetre because of the heat.

     ______

     ______
   - c Sheila discovered that the area of wire mesh needed for the task was 45 square metres.

     ______

     ______
   - d The experiment showed that fifteen hundredths of a cubic metre of gas had escaped in 10 minutes.

     ______

     ______

3. **Write** these **dates** and **times** in the correct form.
   - a the third day of September 2009 ______
   - b a quarter to ten in the evening ______
   - c seven minutes past three in the morning ______
   - d nine-thirty-two in the morning ______
   - e the tenth day of the tenth month this year ______
   - f Tuesday the 17th January 2006 ______

Abbreviations, contractions and acronyms

Abbreviations

Abbreviations are **shortened** forms of **words**. They are words abbreviated using the **first letters** and **some others**. A full stop is used at the end of an abbreviation.

Examples

- anniversary ➡ anniv.
- continued ➡ cont.
- equivalent ➡ equiv.
- miscellaneous ➡ misc.
- Sunday ➡ Sun.
- Honourable ➡ Hon.

Contractions

Contractions are **shortened** forms of **words** that begin with the **first letter** of the word and end with the **last letter** of the word. Contractions do not have a full stop at the end.

Examples

- advertisement ➡ advt
- amount ➡ amt
- government ➡ govt
- quarter ➡ qtr
- Avenue ➡ Ave

Acronyms

Acronyms are words formed from the **first letters** of a group of words. They are **pronounced as a single word**. Full stops are not used.

Examples

- Australian and New Zealand Army Corps ➡ Anzac
- Queensland and Northern Territory Aerial Services ➡ Qantas

Initialisms

Initialisms are strings of the **first letters** of a group of words, but each letter is **pronounced separately**. Full stops are not used.

Examples

- Australian Broadcasting Corporation ➡ ABC
- Returned Services League ➡ RSL
- Western Australia ➡ WA
- Eastern Standard Time ➡ EST
- Gross National Product ➡ GNP
- Member of the House of Representatives ➡ MHR

ACTIVITY 6 Using abbreviations, contractions and acronyms

1. **Write** the following in **abbreviated form**. Include **full stops** as required.

a Queensland ______
b Wednesday ______
c paragraph ______
d Colonel ______
e feminine ______
f Northern Territory ______
g including ______
h certificate ______
i Western Standard Time ______
j December ______
k adjective ______
l South Australia ______

2. **Circle** the correct **abbreviated form** from each group of three.

a Australia:	Austa	Aust	Aust.
b estimated time of arrival:	E.T.A.	ETA	ETOA.
c especially:	esp.	esp	espy
d degree:	deg	deg.	dg.
e electronic data processing:	E.D.P.	EDP.	EDP
f following:	fol	fol.	folg.

3. **Write** the correct **abbreviated form** for each of the following. Insert **full stops** as required.

a anonymous ______
b Company ______
c forward ______
d balance ______
e singular ______
f excluding ______
g approximately ______
h and so on ______
i longitude ______
j received ______

4. **Write** out these acronyms **in full**.

a RSVP ______
b OHMS ______
c CBD ______
d UNICEF ______
e AGM ______
f NESB ______

Direct and indirect speech—quotation marks

Direct or quoted speech

The **actual words spoken** are placed in **quotation marks** ('…'). A full stop, comma, question mark or exclamation mark is placed after the last word spoken.

Examples

- He answered abruptly, 'I do not know.'
- 'What are you doing?' asked Jane.
- 'It's great fun. I love dancing.'
- 'We shall go soon,' said Juan.
- 'Look out!' Ava shouted.

In handwritten text, **additional quotation marks** are used when the name of a book, song, property, homestead or house is used **within quotation marks**. Double quotation marks are placed around the name. In typed text, italics are used.

Examples

- 'Wayne bought a speedboat called "Intruder" yesterday,' she said. (handwritten)
- 'The book *Robinson Crusoe* is a very exciting one!' exclaimed Steve. (typed)

Sometimes direct or quoted speech is divided into **two segments**. Two sets of quotation marks are used. Commas are used to separate the segments.

Examples

'Those crops,' said the producer, 'grow well all year round.'

'Do you really think,' asked Kate, 'that I could do that?'

Indirect or reported speech

When we **report what has been said** we are using indirect or reported speech. The word *that* is generally used before the reported words.

Examples

- Emily said (that) she had to go.
- They told him (that) he should not be late again.
- The officer yelled (that) it was time to move out.

Using indirect speech means that:

- the words spoken are being **reported**
- the sentence is now in the **past tense**
- the **actual words** of the speaker are **not used**.

Comparing direct and indirect speech

Compare these two sentences:

Direct: 'I will go,' said Ellen. **Indirect:** Ellen said (that) she would go.

To change from direct to indirect speech it is sometimes necessary to include the word *that*.

Example

Direct speech		Indirect speech
Amy said, '**I** thought it could be done.'	→	Amy said (**that**) **she** thought it could be done.

ACTIVITY 7 Using direct and indirect speech —quotation marks

1. **Insert quotation marks** and **other punctuation marks** in these sentences.
   - a When will you be able to finish it the supervisor asked
   - b No she said I will not collect the parcel
   - c Look cried the boy you have broken it
   - d Come on said John it needs to be done quickly
   - e The young girl whimpered I know Ive lost it

2. Are these sentences direct or indirect speech? **Tick** (✓) the correct box.

	Direct	Indirect
a The man replied that he had been to the dentist.	☐	☐
b 'Where did you put my axe?' asked the woodman.	☐	☐
c The woman complained that the boat was uncomfortable.	☐	☐

3. a **Write** a sentence using *where have you been* in **direct speech**.

   ____

   ____

   b **Write** a sentence using *that he had not done it* in **indirect speech**.

   ____

   ____

4. **Change** these sentences into **indirect speech**.
   - a 'I have never been to Lake Eyre before,' said the traveller.

   ____

   ____

   - b 'Those hills are very steep, especially in the north,' explained the old timer.

   ____

   ____

5. **Change** these sentences into **direct speech**.
   - a Maddie asked the tall stranger the way to the post office.

   ____

   ____

   - b Some of the students announced that they were going to the football.

   ____

   ____

   - c The teacher explained that the divisor in the operation was twenty-three.

   ____

   ____

ACTIVITY 8 Chapter check

1 **Rewrite** these conversations, **punctuating** them correctly.

a Will you follow the track asked Jim its a long way but the scenery is beautiful look out for snakes on the way i certainly will replied jay

b An employer was interviewing a young lady and had almost completed his discussion with her finally he said do you have any religious views well said the girl i cant say i have but i do have some good pictures of Sydney Harbour and Luna Park

2 **Write** these phrases in a different form using an **apostrophe**.

a the tail of the donkey
b the dresses of the girls
c the marbles belonging to the boy
d the jobs of the workmen
e the coats of the princes
f the books of the mother

3 **Write** these sentences in **direct speech**.

a Tom told Jack he was going to collect his books before nine o'clock on Saturday morning.

b Evan informed his friend John of his plan to travel to Armidale during the May vacation.

4 **Rewrite** these sentences, **adding** correct **punctuation**.

a Where do you think Fairdale is located enquired the salesman

b did carol and michelle read the book sea rescue during the may holidays asked the librarian

c have you ever heard the band play st louis blues asked the soldier

Part B

Focus on improving your writing

In these chapters you will learn to improve the construction of your sentences and develop your paragraphing skills. You will also learn about setting a scene and creating word pictures.

5 Writing better sentences

In this chapter you will learn to write **more interesting sentences**.

Basic sentences are those that have as **few words** as a sentence can have. Here are five basic sentences.

1. Lions roared. (noun–verb)
2. Dogs eat meat. (noun–verb–noun)
3. Children become adults. (noun–linking verb–noun)
4. Artists are clever. (noun–linking verb–adjective)
5. Adults give children presents. (noun–verb–noun–noun)

Constructing longer sentences

Writers use basic sentences to **construct longer sentences** and **paragraphs**. They **build** expressive and interesting sentences by **adding** single words and groups of words to the basic sentence.

Example

Lions roared.  Charging forward, the two golden maned young **lions roared** loudly to startle the intruders away.

Task

Can you **match** these more expressive sentences to the basic types 1–5 listed above? For example, for a noun–verb–noun basic sentence, write *2*.

- Many small **fish swim** in the stream. ________
- Some of our **relatives were soldiers** in the last war. ________
- Many of the **trainers provided** excellent **instructions** to the athletes. ________
- Several large **pictures** on the wall **were** very **attractive**. ________
- The huge sparkling white **avalanche smothered** the group of **climbers**. ________

Adding detail

Writers can **add more detail** to a basic sentence by adding words and phrases that tell **when**, **where**, **why** or **how**.

Example

Dogs ate meat. ➡ The pack of savage **dogs ate** the discarded **meat** within a few minutes.

Many **different types of words** are used in sentence building. The **articles** (the three words *a*, *an* and *the*) occur regularly in many sentences. In this chapter you will look at some other types of words, phrases and clauses that can be used to build expressive sentences.

Adding adjectives and adjectival phrases

- An **adjective** is a **describing word**. It tells us what kind of, how many, how much or which person or object is being described.
- An **adjectival phrase** tells us about a noun or pronoun and, therefore, does the work of an adjective. These phrases do not contain a finite verb and usually begin with a **preposition**.

Examples

- **The car sped along.**

Adding adjectives and/or adjectival phrases, the sentence could become:

The neat, red sports car with its headlights blazing sped along the track.

The low-slung, racing car with bright red and green markings sped along the narrow, winding road.

- **A horse galloped quickly.**

Adding adjectives and/or adjectival phrases the sentence could become:

A thoroughbred bay horse with a white blaze galloped quickly.

A strong, Arabian horse with decorated saddle and reins galloped quickly.

Task

Build expressive sentences by **selecting adjectives** and **adjectival phrases** from these lists and **adding** them to the sentences below.

Adjectives

several	many	numerous	talented	clever	humorous
neatly dressed	entertaining	spectacular	unusual	playful	well-fed

Adjectival phrases

in the green dress	with long dark hair	of world standard	of great skill
with a black cloak	in the checked shirt	of various sizes	with woolly coats
from interstate	with pink ears		

1. Young animals grazed there.

2. The girl became a pianist.

3. The magician gave the boy a rabbit.

Adding adverbs and adverbial phrases

- An **adverb** is a word that tells us about or **modifies other words** such as verbs, adjectives and other adverbs. Many adverbs tell how, when or where.
- An **adverbial phrase** is a group of words without a finite verb. An adverbial phrase tells us about a verb and does the work of an adverb. Adverbial phrases usually begin with a **preposition**.

Examples

- **The fish swam.**

Adding adverbs or adverbial phrases, the sentence could become:

The fish swam lazily across the pond to the rocky edges.

The fish swam strongly in an anti-clockwise direction towards the feeding zone.

- **Several pictures were arranged.**

Adding adverbs and/or adverbial phrases, the sentence could become:

Several pictures were carefully arranged in an artistic way to reflect the owner's personality.

Several pictures were tastefully arranged in the narrow gallery for the visitors' enjoyment.

Task

Build expressive sentences by selecting **adverbs** and **adverbial phrases** from these lists and adding them to the sentences below.

Adverbs

slowly, quickly, badly, seriously, then, instantly, seriously, nearly, effortlessly, now, again

Adverbial phrases

in the morning, at dusk, by the vehicles, during the day, in a careful manner, without delay, by midday, after the storm

1. Several birds were injured.

2. The boys painted the fence.

3. The young girl climbed the hill.

ACTIVITY 1 Building expressive sentences

Build expressive sentences using the lists below. **Add** at least one **adjective**, one **adverb**, one **adjectival phrase** and one **adverbial phrase** to each of the sentences below.

Adjectives

playful	injured	delightful	fluffy	white	experienced
hard-working	exhausted	weary	young	cheerful	famished
hungry	frost-bitten	tall	handsome	kind	pleasant
agreeable	excited	overjoyed	older	delighted	several

Adverbs

kindly	selfishly	quietly	nervously	easily	quickly
soon	reluctantly	noisily	happily	excitedly	ravenously
deliberately	hastily	cautiously	hungrily	greedily	

Adjectival phrases

with the tawny coats	in grey work clothes	in uniform	with red bows
with work-worn hands	in a blue shirt	in the cage	from Adelaide
in school uniform	with their pets	with a beard	in ragged clothes
over eight years old	in a bright green suit		

Adverbial phrases

up and down the curtain	after three o'clock	at once	by the steps
after much searching	after the parade	with great speed	by the lake
with great enjoyment	with the ball of string	early in the day	before lunch
near the chaff-cutter	in a cautious manner	at the concert	in the lounge

1. The stranger gave the visitor a fifty-cent coin.

____

____

____

2. The boys ate the food.

____

____

____

3. The farmer found the bags.

____

____

____

4. Students left the school.

____

____

Adding participle and verbal noun phrases

- A **participle phrase** is a group of words without a finite verb. The phrase does the work of an **adjective**.
- A **verbal noun phrase** is a group of words without a finite verb. The phrase does the work of a **noun**.

Examples

- **The car sped away.**

Adding a participle phrase the sentence could become:

The car travelling at high speed sped away.
The car powered by the new engine sped away.

- **The boys liked stamps.**

Adding a verbal noun phrase the sentence could become:

The boys liked collecting Australian and overseas stamps.
The boys liked collecting many different types of stamps.

Task

Build expressive sentences by selecting **participle** or **verbal noun phrases** from these lists and including them in the sentences below.

Participle phrases

developed over many years
followed for some time
wearing the blue outfit
enjoyed by many people
dressed in red and white

Verbal noun phrases

weight training with her friends
competing in marathons
speeding along the forest tracks
attempting long races
lifting weights at the gym
jogging through the forest
racing on his new bike
riding trail bikes

1. His favourite pastime was trail bike riding.

2. The girl enjoyed training.

3. Running is a great hobby.

Adding infinitive phrases

An **infinitive phrase** begins with an infinitive (e.g. *to eat*, *to run*, *to finish*).

Example

- **The cat was over there.**

Adding an infinitive phrase, the sentence could become:

The cat to be taken to the vet is over there.

The cat to star in the advertisement is over there.

Task 1

Build expressive sentences by **selecting infinitive phrases** from the list to **add to** the sentences below.

Infinitive phrases

to complete the project
to advise the architect
to help with the work
to take to the race track
to be repaired
to re-paint

1. The car is by the shed. ______
2. The artists gathered in the lobby. ______

Task 2

Build expressive sentences by **including** suitable **participle**, **verbal noun** or **infinitive phrases** from the lists below.

Participle phrases

waiting at the gate
resting near the wall
entering the building
wearing a blue dress
lying on the deck

Verbal noun phrases

enjoying the celebration
breaking the rules
fixing the old machines
catching strange and colourful insects

Infinitive phrases

to celebrate her birthday
to repair the item
to be erected
to enter the exhibit
to be bandaged

1. The animals ran away.
______
2. The girl arrived.
______
3. The worker enjoyed the machinery.
______

Adding adjectival and adverbial clauses

- An **adjectival clause** describes a noun or pronoun in one of the other clauses in a sentence. Adjectival clauses **begin with** *who*, *whom*, *whose*, *which* and *that*.
- An **adverbial clause** does the work of an adverb. It tells how, when, where or why an action takes place. It begins with a **conjunction**.

Examples

- **The dog was at the gate.**

Adding an adjectival clause, the sentence could become:

The dog, which I have owned for many years, was at the gate.
The dog was at the gate that had recently been replaced.

Adding an adverbial clause, the sentence could become:

The dog was at the gate when we woke up.
The dog was at the gate because he was injured.

- **The boy ran away.**

Adding an adverbial clause, the sentence could become:

The boy ran away as if he were very frightened.
When the bell rang the boy ran away.
The boy ran away where no one could possibly find him.

Task

Build expressive sentences using suitable **adjectival** or **adverbial clauses** from the lists below.

Adjectival clauses

which had been re-painted
who attended Macgregor College
who had come from interstate
that had been along the track
of whom I spoke

Adverbial clauses

after the sun had gone down
while the parents arranged the ceremony
because they had time to spare
when they arrived early on Friday
when the work had been completed

1. The students played.

2. The car appeared.

3. The visitors toured the park.

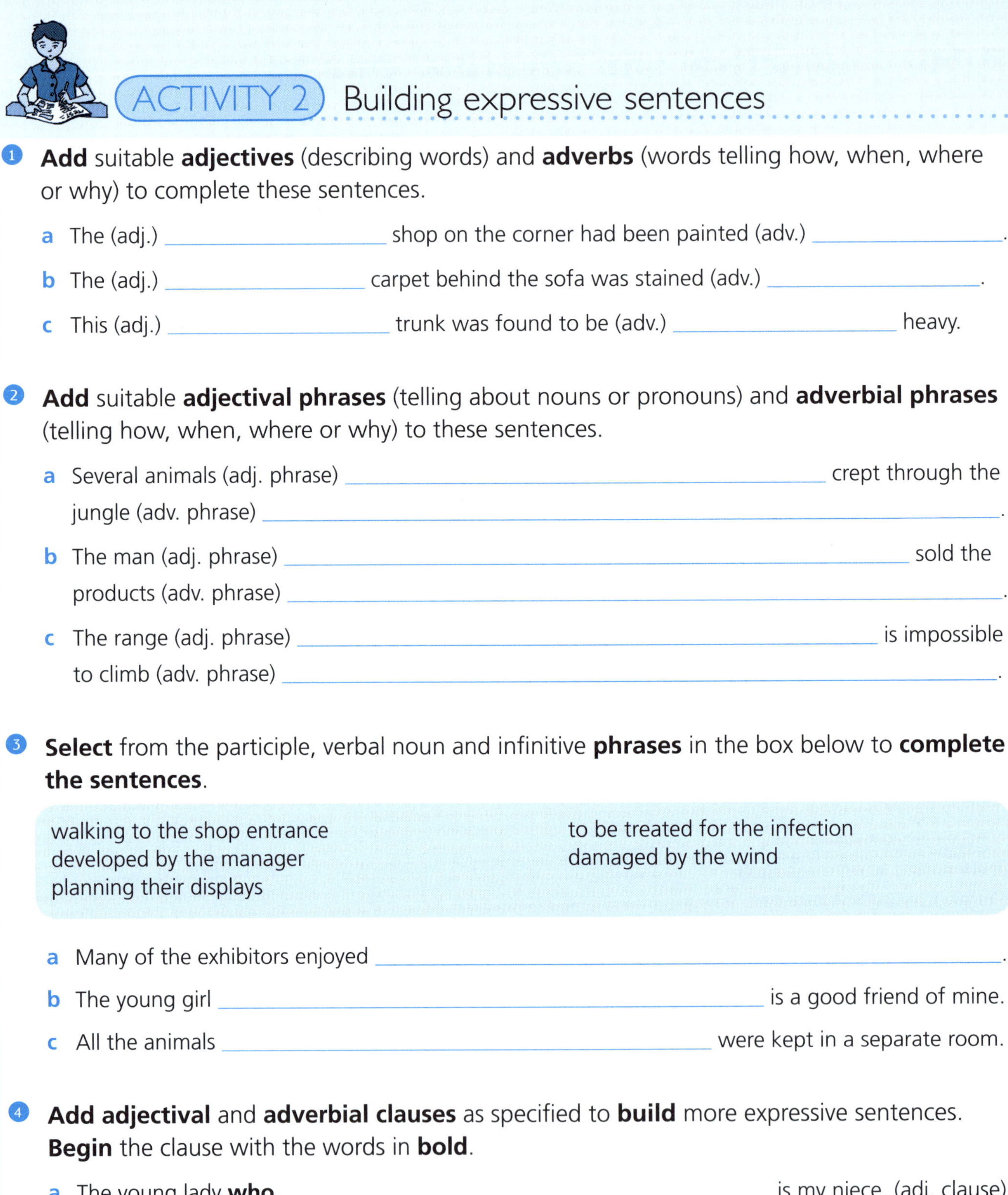

ACTIVITY 2 Building expressive sentences

1. **Add** suitable **adjectives** (describing words) and **adverbs** (words telling how, when, where or why) to complete these sentences.

   a The (adj.) ____________ shop on the corner had been painted (adv.) ____________.

   b The (adj.) ____________ carpet behind the sofa was stained (adv.) ____________.

   c This (adj.) ____________ trunk was found to be (adv.) ____________ heavy.

2. **Add** suitable **adjectival phrases** (telling about nouns or pronouns) and **adverbial phrases** (telling how, when, where or why) to these sentences.

   a Several animals (adj. phrase) ____________________ crept through the jungle (adv. phrase) ____________________.

   b The man (adj. phrase) ____________________ sold the products (adv. phrase) ____________________.

   c The range (adj. phrase) ____________________ is impossible to climb (adv. phrase) ____________________.

3. **Select** from the participle, verbal noun and infinitive **phrases** in the box below to **complete the sentences**.

walking to the shop entrance	to be treated for the infection
developed by the manager	damaged by the wind
planning their displays	

   a Many of the exhibitors enjoyed ____________________.

   b The young girl ____________________ is a good friend of mine.

   c All the animals ____________________ were kept in a separate room.

4. **Add adjectival** and **adverbial clauses** as specified to **build** more expressive sentences. **Begin** the clause with the words in **bold**.

   a The young lady **who** ____________________ is my niece. (adj. clause)

   b All the animals will be transported away **when** ____________________. (adv. clause)

   c The celebrity **who** ____________________ (adj. clause) presented the trophy to the winner **because** ____________________ (adv. clause).

   d **If** ____________________ (adv. clause) the mountaineer's gear, **which** ____________________ (adj. clause), will be packed carefully.

Sentence variety

Basic sentences can be **joined** to make more interesting sentences. Look at this example.

Example

Peter went to the dentist.
It was quickly attended to.
He had a bad toothache.
He returned home.

These four sentences could be **combined** into one or two sentences. Here is one way of doing this.

- Peter had a bad toothache and he went to the dentist and it was quickly attended to and he returned home.

Here the word *and* was used three times to combine the sentences. The word *and* should be **used sparingly** to combine sentences. Here are two **more expressive** ways.

- Peter, suffering from a bad toothache, visited the dentist where it was quickly attended to before he went home.
- After his bad toothache was attended to by the dentist, Peter returned home.

Task

Combine these groups of sentences.

1. Sue studied the map.
   She travelled along High Street.
   She turned down Jane Street.
   She finally reached Sandra's house.

   ____

   ____

2. Max found the rabbit.
   It had escaped.
   It was hiding near the shed.
   He carried it back to the owner.

   ____

   ____

   ____

3. They admired the car.
   It had just arrived.
   It was a brilliant white colour.
   Others came to see the car.

   ____

   ____

   ____

   ____

4. The track was very steep.
   Loose rocks made it dangerous.
   Extreme care needed to be taken.
   The travellers were very cautious.

   ____

   ____

   ____

   ____

Changing sentence form

One way to improve your writing is to use a **variety** of **sentence forms**.

The three sentences in each group below express the **same thought** but in **different forms**.

Examples

- The colourful butterflies flew slowly to the higher branches.
- To the higher branches the colourful butterflies flew slowly.
- Slowly, the colourful butterflies flew to the higher branches.

- The weary explorers trudged blindly into the dark opening in the rocks.
- Into the dark opening in the rocks the weary explorers trudged blindly.
- Blindly, the weary explorers trudged into the dark opening in the rocks.

Task

Rewrite each sentence below **twice** in different forms, starting with the words given.

1. The tiny creature that had been trapped now cleverly escaped through the narrow opening.
   - **a** Through the narrow opening ____________________
   - **b** Now ____________________

2. The escapee injured by the fall crawled through the darkness towards the abandoned cabin at dusk.
   - **a** Towards the abandoned cabin ____________________
   - **b** At dusk ____________________

3. The beautiful tawny Abyssinian cat curled itself up and immediately fell asleep close to the fireplace.
   - **a** Close to the fireplace ____________________
   - **b** Curling itself up ____________________

4. The riders, almost blanketed by the dense fog, increased speed on the downhill run.
   - **a** Almost blanketed ____________________
   - **b** On the downhill run ____________________

Avoiding repetition

Using **different words** to **start sentences** will make your writing more interesting.

Task 1

Read the passage below and **follow** the directions.

There were many people at the station. There were young people and adults waiting quietly. They sat on the long seats on the platform. There were some who were reading. They seemed the most relaxed of all. There were others who were quite impatient.

1. **Underline** the **first word** in each sentence.

   Write the words. ______________________________

   This is quite a dull group of sentences as it lacks variety. The words *there* and *they* have been repeated throughout. Now **read** the passage that has been rewritten so that it has more variety in sentence construction.

Many, many people could be seen at the station. Young people and adults were waiting quietly for their train to arrive. Sitting on the long seats on the platform, many travellers enjoyed reading while they waited. It was plain to see that these people were the most relaxed. Others, tired of the long wait, were obviously quite impatient.

2. **Underline** the **first word** in each sentence.

   Write the words. ______________________________

   You will see that the words at the beginning of the sentences and the structure of the sentences are now **different**. This is a much more interesting piece of writing, because the writer **avoided repetition**.

Task 2

Read the next example and again follow the directions.

Laura had enjoyed travelling to the city. She first went into the large department store. Laura wanted to buy several presents for her relatives. She spent an hour in the toy section. She hoped to buy some interesting new toys for her brothers. Laura was amazed at the huge variety of toys. She then went on to the clothing section.

Underline the **first word** in each sentence.

Write the words. ______________________________

Again, this is quite a dull group of sentences, as it lacks variety. The words *Laura* and *she* have been used as the first word in each of the sentences.

Now **read** the passage that has been rewritten so that it has more variety in sentence construction.

Laura had quite enjoyed travelling to the big city. Her first stop was the large department store in the centre of town. Hoping to buy several presents for her relatives, she first found the section for toys. Her brothers had asked her to look at some newly created toys, which they had noticed in the store's catalogue. An amazing array of sparkling new toys made an attractive display. After making several purchases Laura moved on to the clothing section.

Again, this is a much brighter piece of writing as the writer has avoided repetition.

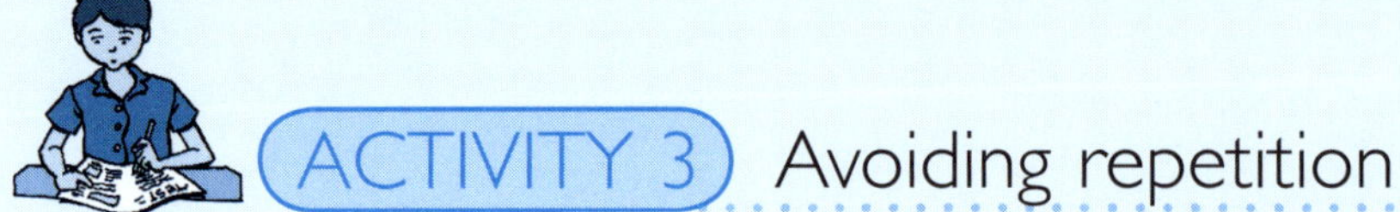

ACTIVITY 3 Avoiding repetition

- **Read** the following groups of sentences and note the lack of sentence variety.
- **Rewrite** the sentences so that the pieces of writing are brighter and more interesting.
- **Add** any **words**, **phrases** or **clauses** necessary to improve them.

1. Allan and Rod were enjoying a holiday with their aunt and uncle. They had begun visiting many years ago. Alan and Rod really enjoyed the holiday cottage. They often left in the early morning to explore the coves and caves below the holiday home. Alan and Rod often spent all day on the beach and around the cliff. They always enjoyed watching the sun go down from the back deck.

2. Sanchia and her friends decided to go camping on Friday Island. They set out with their camping gear in their small outboard. It was a fine day and the sea was very calm. The island was only eight kilometres from their home. They secured their boat and carried their gear ashore. They then had to decide on a suitable campsite. They checked out several areas. They found a sheltered spot and carried all their gear over to it. It was near a fresh water spring and near a large swimming hole.

ACTIVITY 4 Building expressive sentences

1 **Combine** this group of sentences into **one sentence**.

Jason went to the village.

He went to the produce store.

He bought some food for the pony.

He also bought a new halter.

____

____

____

____

2 Four sentences were combined and the result is given in the box. **Improve** the sentence by **avoiding** the use of *and*.

> The box was found in the lunchroom and Sharon had found it and took it home and showed it to her parents.

____

____

____

3 **Rewrite** the sentence in the box **twice**, **beginning with** the **words given**.

> Many of the animals that had been injured in the fire were treated carefully by the wildlife personnel at the centre.

a At the centre ______________________________

____

b Carefully ______________________________

____

4 **Read** the following group of sentences. **Rewrite** it so that it becomes a brighter and more interesting piece of writing. **Add** any **words**, **phrases** or **clauses** necessary to improve it.

> The visitors arrived at the zoo at nine o'clock. They lined up in the long queue and were inside the main gates in twenty minutes. The visitors took the opportunity to enjoy a cup of coffee before studying the map of the zoo. They all wanted to look at the new polar bear enclosure. All of them decided to go there first. It was about three hundred metres from the coffee shop.

____

____

____

____

____

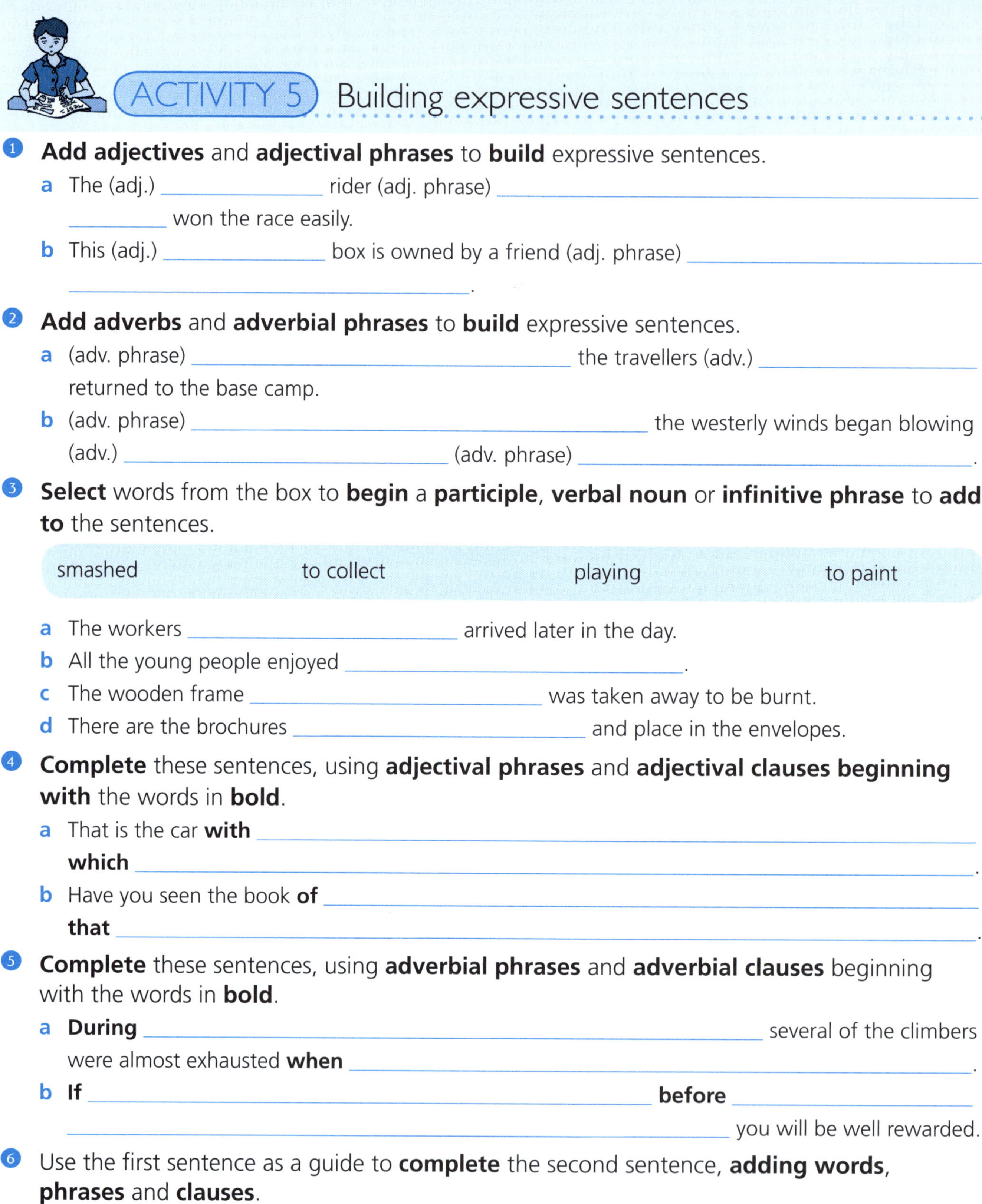

ACTIVITY 5 Building expressive sentences

1 **Add adjectives** and **adjectival phrases** to **build** expressive sentences.

a The (adj.) ______________ rider (adj. phrase) ______________________________ __________ won the race easily.

b This (adj.) ______________ box is owned by a friend (adj. phrase) ______________________ ______________________________.

2 **Add adverbs** and **adverbial phrases** to **build** expressive sentences.

a (adv. phrase) ______________________________ the travellers (adv.) ______________ returned to the base camp.

b (adv. phrase) ______________________________ the westerly winds began blowing (adv.) ______________________ (adv. phrase) ______________________________.

3 **Select** words from the box to **begin** a **participle**, **verbal noun** or **infinitive phrase** to **add to** the sentences.

smashed	to collect	playing	to paint

a The workers ______________________ arrived later in the day.

b All the young people enjoyed ______________________________.

c The wooden frame ______________________ was taken away to be burnt.

d There are the brochures ______________________ and place in the envelopes.

4 **Complete** these sentences, using **adjectival phrases** and **adjectival clauses beginning with** the words in **bold**.

a That is the car **with** ______________________________ **which** ______________________________.

b Have you seen the book **of** ______________________________ **that** ______________________________.

5 **Complete** these sentences, using **adverbial phrases** and **adverbial clauses** beginning with the words in **bold**.

a **During** ______________________________ several of the climbers were almost exhausted **when** ______________________________.

b **If** ______________________________ **before** ______________________ ______________________________ you will be well rewarded.

6 Use the first sentence as a guide to **complete** the second sentence, **adding words**, **phrases** and **clauses**.

a Bring me a fine red rose from a bush in the lower garden. Place it (adv.) ______________ in this (adj.) ______________ vase given to me (adv. phrase) ______________ ______________________________ several years ago.

b With the passing of many years the slender oak tree became a huge specimen. Its dense (adj.) ______________ foliage created a (adj.) ______________ resting place for travellers (adj. clause) ______________________________.

ACTIVITY 6 Building expressive sentences

1. **Combine** this group of sentences into **one sentence**.

   The explorers entered the ranges.
   They had journeyed for weeks.
   Supplies were running low.
   They needed to replenish their stores.

2. **Rewrite** the sentence in the box **twice**, **beginning with** the **words given**.

   The group of archers boldly turned to the right of the castle wall and fired into the defenders' ranks.

   a Into the ranks of the defenders

   b Turning to the right

3. **Rewrite** the group of sentences below so that it becomes a brighter and more interesting piece of writing. **Add** any **words**, **phrases** or **clauses** necessary to improve it.

   The labourers came early with all their equipment. They knew it would be a long day. Their task was to complete the drainage trenches. All the men in the group knew the ground was packed hard and would be difficult to dig. They began immediately and soon beads of perspiration were running down their backs. They continued on for three hours and then had a break.

6 Paragraphs

In this chapter you will learn how to **group sentences** together in **paragraphs**.

- **Paragraphs** are **groups of sentences** that are **related**. They work together to provide a clear picture of something, to develop an idea or to recount in sequence a series of events.
- It is easy to recognise paragraphs because they are **indented** or a **space** is left between them.

Task

Read the paragraphs below. Notice the **relationship** between the **sentences**.

The 1929 expedition

In 1929 Dr Douglas Mawson was requested by the Australian Government to organise an expedition to Antarctica. It was to use men and equipment from Australia, Great Britain and New Zealand. The main object of the expedition was to explore the coastline. They were also to try to find anything that might be valuable for their countries, such as minerals. Because of the success of this journey and another two years later, a large part of Antarctica was taken over by Australia. As a result of this, Australia has been able to limit fishing and whaling in this area.

Outline
- Personnel
- Objectives
- Further journey
- Result

Penguins

Penguins are found in the Antarctic region but not in the Arctic. These flightless birds are perfect swimmers and are completely adapted to life in the water. Their wings are used as flippers and their body is covered by a protective layer of blubber. There are many different varieties of penguins. Some live around the cool regions of Africa, Australasia and South America. Others live happily along the warmer coasts of Peru and Chile, and even on the Galapagos Islands just on the Equator. Two types of penguins, the Emperor and the Adelie penguins, are found only on the Antarctic continent and the surrounding islands.

Outline
- Description
- Varieties
- Locations

ACTIVITY 1 Identifying paragraphs

1 The article below is about the Antarctic region and the explorers who first began journeying in this frozen wasteland. There should be three paragraphs:

- The **first paragraph** describes the area and the intense cold.
- The **second paragraph** describes the winds of the region.
- The **third paragraph** introduces the early explorers.

a **Mark** *(1)* where paragraph 1 should end.

b **Mark** *(2)* where paragraph 2 should end.

Antarctica

Antarctica is a lost continent, lost under a huge solid ice cap. This massive ice cap is over five kilometres thick in places and covers an area bigger than Australia and Europe put together. In the upland regions of Antarctica the cold is so intense that it freezes the air into a crystal-like greyish-white mist. The biting winds that whistle across the frozen plains harden the brittle ice. The winds from the polar plateaux are even worse. These terrifyingly cold rivers of heavy air rush down the frozen slopes and howl across the plains in savage gusts up to 250 kilometres per hour. Winds such as these can lift heavy objects, hurl them along and knock people completely over. Carrying along snowflakes, ice crystals and frozen lumps of ice, these are the most dangerous winds in the world. In the early part of this century, scientists and explorers were becoming very interested in this forgotten continent. Men such as Sir Robert Scott, Ernest Shackleton and Roald Amundsen, through their journeys in this frozen wasteland, increased our knowledge.

2 The article below is about middle distance running. There should be three paragraphs:

- **paragraph 1** about middle distance running and style
- **paragraph 2** about training
- **paragraph 3** about tactics.

a **Mark** *(1)* where paragraph 1 should end.

b **Mark** *(2)* where paragraph 2 should end.

Middle distance running

Middle distance running is one of the most interesting branches of track athletics. For young athletes, the usual distances are 800 metres and 1500 metres. Style of running is very important. Your running should be relaxed and your arm and leg movements must use a lot less energy than in a sprint. In middle distance races you are concerned with saving, or conserving, energy. Training to handle middle distance running is essential. A good middle distance runner needs to be able to run fast and maintain speed for the whole of the race. As well, a good finish is needed. To do this you need to build up your heart, lungs and legs so that they can work efficiently over the whole race. Build up your stamina by even paced steady runs over short distances and then increase the distances. In middle distance running, tactics are important. In the race itself tactics means avoiding common mistakes and making the best possible use of your position in the race. Always make sure that you do not run wide at the turns. Make sure that you get yourself into a good position as soon as you start. Try to avoid being boxed in but, if you are, it is usually possible to move out on a turn.

Reorganising paragraphs

Sentences about the **same topic** should be in the **same paragraph**.

Task 1

Read the article below. There should be **three** paragraphs:

- **paragraph A**: Cobb and Co. and expansion
- **paragraph B**: passengers and freight
- **paragraph C**: bushranger problems.

Decide which paragraph each sentence belongs to. **Write the number** of each sentence against the proper paragraph.

Paragraph A: ______________________

Paragraph B: ______________________

Paragraph C: ______________________

Early transport

1 During the early years of European settlement in Australia horses played a key role. **2** They were used to haul wagons and coaches across the ranges onto the western plains. **3** The coaches were often held up by a single bushranger or a group of outlaws. **4** The most famous of the Australian coach lines was Cobb and Co. **5** This company began operating from Melbourne in 1853. **6** Building materials, food supplies and household goods were transported to the towns while products for export were brought from the towns to the ports. **7** By 1870 Cobb and Co. had 6000 horses in harness each day and travelled 45 000 kilometres a week. **8** It was gold that created, or at least increased, the level of bushranging in the colonies. **9** The gold discoveries caused a rapid increase in coach services. **10** Bushrangers would often rob the passengers of any valuables they were carrying. **11** The coaches and wagons carried passengers and freight—passengers to and from the developing towns and all kinds of freight. **12** Although a colonial police force was established, the bushrangers flourished in many areas.

Task 2

Now you have allocated the sentences to the correct paragraphs, **consider** the **order** of the **sentences** in each paragraph. Would the sentences be more effective in a slightly different order? If so, **write** the **correct order** of sentences for each paragraph.

Paragraph A: ______________________

Paragraph B: ______________________

Paragraph C: ______________________

ACTIVITY 2 Reorganising paragraphs

This short article contains ten sentences. It should be divided into **three paragraphs**:

- **paragraph 1**: the game of squash
- **paragraph 2**: international federation
- **paragraph 3**: an Australian champion.

Rewrite the article, placing the sentences in the **correct order**.

The game of squash

- Squash has become a very popular sport in Australia.
- Many countries agreed to play according to international rules.
- Heather Blundell displayed great skill at hockey, tennis and squash.
- The game of squash is an indoor one, a little like handball.
- Heather won the junior and senior titles at the age of seventeen.
- In squash, racquets and a hard rubber ball are used.
- In the 1960s an international federation of countries playing squash was set up.
- Heather went on to become one of the greatest female squash players of all time.
- Nine countries, including Australia, joined the international federation.
- The players use racquets to hit the ball against any of the four walls of the court.

Sequence of paragraphs

In paragraphs that describe a **series** of events or actions the **sequence** or order of sentences in the paragraph is important.

- The **main idea** is usually in the **first sentence**.
- The remaining sentences are in the **order** in which the **events occurred**.

Example

It was the day of the Devonport Cup, a horse race over 2100 metres. All the best horses from far and wide had come to race in the event. The racetrack was firm but it was drizzling rain as the race began. At the beginning the favourite, Benair, was in the lead. All through to the 1500 metre mark the field was tightly packed. Benair was under pressure from four other horses. Gradually the unknown Tewala crept up beside Benair and then accelerated away. At the bend, with 600 metres to travel, Tewala held a lead of three lengths. In the straight Benair and Tewala were neck and neck. With one hundred metres to go Tewala surged ahead for a great win, with Benair in second place.

Task

Read the sets of sentences and decide on the **correct sequence**. **Write** the sentence **numbers** in the boxes below, in the correct order.

A
1 There in the centre of the clearing was a magnificent stag.
2 He knew he would have to move a little closer to be sure of an accurate shot.
3 The young hunter stood perfectly still at the edge of the clearing.
4 Suddenly, the hunter brushed against a thin branch, which caused a slight cracking sound.
5 The stag turned and instantly plunged forwards to escape once again.
6 Almost soundlessly, the hunter advanced slowly towards the edge of the clearing.

☐ ☐ ☐ ☐ ☐ ☐

B
1 Alan and Jalna were enjoying their holiday at their relatives' cottage on the edge of the cliff.
2 The small craft was soon up on the sandy beach.
3 The teenagers noticed four rough looking men begin unloading two crates from the boat.
4 Before dawn the teenagers wandered down the path that led to the edge of the cliffs.
5 In silence, they carried the crates to the base of the cliff.
6 Just as the sun rose they noticed a small boat gliding quietly into the bay beneath the cliff.

☐ ☐ ☐ ☐ ☐ ☐

Topic sentences and main ideas

- Each paragraph has a **topic sentence**.
- The topic sentence contains the **main idea**. All the other information in a paragraph is called the **supporting detail**.
- **Paragraph types** can **vary** according to the **text type**.

Paragraph type A

- The **topic sentence** is the **first** sentence.
- The **main idea** is in **this sentence**.
- The rest is **supporting detail**.

On a cool autumn day in April 1452, one of the greatest artists of all time—Leonardo da Vinci—was born. His father, Piero da Vinci, was a lawyer who lived in the small village of Vinci, in a region known as Tuscany, in Italy. The Vinci family had lived there for generations. Piero's forefathers had been lawyers and had gradually built up the da Vinci fortunes.

Paragraph type B

- There are **two topic sentences**.
- The **main idea** is in the **first sentence**.
- The main idea is **re-stated** in the last sentence with **more emphasis**.

On 15 July 1606 Rembrandt, the greatest of all Dutch painters, was born. He was the eighth child of Harmen and Cornelia van Rijn—Harmen was a miller and Cornelia was the daughter of a baker. The family lived in the city of Leyden on the banks of the Rhine River. **Rembrandt's great artistic skills, particularly his ability as a portrait painter and his treatment of light and shade, have never been equalled.**

Paragraph type C

- There is **one topic sentence**.
- The **main idea** is in the **topic sentence**.
- The **topic sentence** is placed neither at the **beginning** nor at the **end** of the **paragraph**.

Charles Kingsford-Smith had many different flying opportunities. He thought he would have to work out a way of showing the world what great things aircraft could do. **Smithy decided that a great achievement, such as flying across the Pacific Ocean from the United States to Australia, would be one way of showing the world just how important aircraft would become.** Most people considered the idea terribly dangerous and quite hopeless. At the time most people did not share Kingsford-Smith's confidence in aircraft.

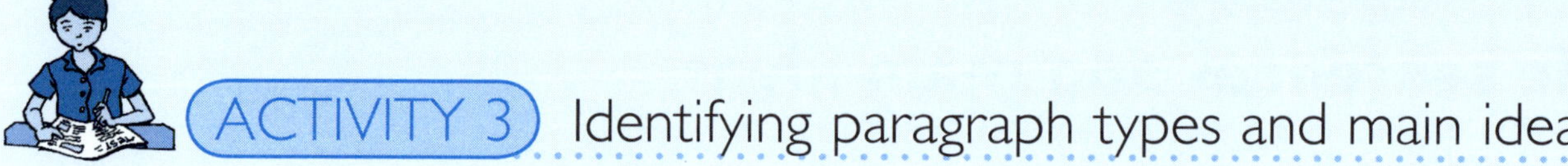

ACTIVITY 3 Identifying paragraph types and main ideas

- **Read** the paragraphs on this page.
- Identify and **underline** the **topic sentence**.
- **Indicate** the paragraph as **type A**, **B** or **C**, as shown on the previous page.

1 Sports in Tudor England

Many different types of sport were practised in England during the Tudor period of history. Outdoor sports, such as wrestling, football, tennis and hockey, were played in many places. The rich landowners often enjoyed hunting and hawking. The most common sport was archery and every fit male was expected to practise on Sunday mornings. People also went to watch brutal forms of entertainment, such as bear baiting and bull baiting. These events involved the bear or bull being tied up and attacked by a number of dogs.

Type of paragraph: ______

2 The slave trade

The African slave trade was one of the most inhuman and shameful activities in which many countries participated. When the Spanish first created settlements in the Americas they sent to Africa for Negro workers. Many traders set up slave markets to satisfy the market. The African people were captured, brought to central locations and then sent to the Americas. Conditions were harsh and cruel and the countries involved were condemned for their role in this terrible example of inhumanity.

Type of paragraph: ______

3 The discovery of radium

Madame Marie Curie, born in Poland, became a great scientist and was honoured by most countries for her work on the discovery of radium. Marie was a very clever girl who excelled in her schoolwork. After moving to Paris she enrolled in the Paris University and studied for a Masters Degree in science. She married Pierre Curie in 1895 and their life together added to the store of medical knowledge. In 1903 Madame Curie received the Nobel Prize for physics and she was appointed a lecturer at the University of Paris.

Type of paragraph: ______

4 Herb Elliott—champion runner

Herb Elliott was born in Perth in 1938. At school he was an outstanding athlete, playing top class football and winning a variety of athletics events. After leaving school at the age of seventeen he won the 800 metre and 1500 metre events and seemed set for further success. It was in 1956 that Herb was inspired with a fierce determination to become one of our greatest runners—it was a turning point in his life. At the 1956 Olympic Games in Melbourne he watched the ruthless approach and great running style of the Russian Vladimir Kuts, who won the 5000 and 10 000 metre events.

Type of paragraph: ______

ACTIVITY 4 Identifying main ideas

Read these paragraphs. **Underline** the **topic sentence** with the main idea.

1 **Running**

In the Olympic Games the longest race of all is called the marathon. The race begins in the centre track of the Olympic Stadium. The runners then go out onto the roads to complete the race, which is over 42 kilometres. The race ends with the runners coming back into the stadium to run one final lap of the running track.

2 **The Indian brave**

He was dressed in his ceremonial clothing. He wore deerskin leggings and moccasins. There were four eagle feathers tied together over his left shoulder. As he stood there in the bright sunlight, this powerfully built man was an impressive sight. He carried a lance about two metres long. His buffalo hide shield had a moon design on it.

3 **Christopher Columbus**

Christopher Columbus, the son of a weaver in Genoa, became the greatest sailor of his time. He was always interested in the sea. He became a skilful seaman and made many short voyages. At first he travelled down the west coast of Africa. After reading the book *The Travels of Marco Polo*, he was sure that the world was round. What he wanted to do was to find a way to China by sailing west.

4 **Carracks**

In the time of Columbus there were many types of small vessels. One was called the carrack. The main vessel used by Columbus when he discovered the Americas was the *Santa Maria*, the most famous carrack of all. She was about twenty-five metres long and about eight metres wide. She had three masts and five sails and could travel well in very shallow water.

5 **Bernborough**

One of Australia's greatest champion racehorses was Bernborough. He was bred near Oakey and raced at tracks around Toowoomba in Queensland. The horse won several races and was seen as a future champion. He was trained for important races in Brisbane, Sydney and Melbourne. He was soon a favourite with race goers. This great horse won fifteen races in a row. In his last race he damaged a bone in one leg and could never race again. Bernborough, through his great ability and will to win, became a racing legend.

ACTIVITY 5 Identifying main ideas

Read these paragraphs**. Identify** the **topic sentence** with the **main idea** and **write** the **topic sentence** below the passage.

1 The quarter horse

The quarter horse is probably the youngest breed of horse in America. In the early days of the settlement of America, racing horses was a popular sport. The horses ran over a distance of about 440 yards. This was a quarter of a mile, so the horses became known as quarter horses. Nowadays, the quarter horse is a very useful animal. It is a very good horse for working with cattle. It is used for racing over short distances and is a very good horse for rodeo work. Some people think that the quarter horse can do more jobs better than any horse in the world.

2 Strange visitors

The Caribs and the Arawaks lived on the islands of the West Indies for centuries. The weather was almost always warm and fine and the people lived a contented life, as had their forefathers. The big changes began after 1492, when some Arawaks living on a small island in the Bahamas saw three ships lying off shore. These were the ships of Christopher Columbus. The Arawaks watched as the strange ships came closer and men came ashore from them. The puzzled Arawaks had never seen such men as these with their beards, strange clothes and bright metal weapons.

3 Climbing Mt Everest

The dangers of a climb to the top of Mt Everest are immense. The icefalls, avalanches, thin ice over unseen crevasses and the risk of falling when climbing are the obvious ones. Other problems, caused by climbing at high altitudes, pose serious threats for mountaineers. The low atmospheric pressure at high altitudes means that the body receives less oxygen than it normally requires. The result is often called mountain sickness, with symptoms being weakness, nausea, sleeplessness and headache. Another major difficulty to be overcome is protection against severe cold. On the top slopes of Everest, the temperature can drop to minus 40°C. Without effective and reliable cold-weather protective clothing, survival in this hostile environment is impossible.

Identifying main ideas and supporting details

A paragraph contains:

- **one main idea**
- **supporting details**.

George Bass

George Bass and his companion Matthew Flinders were important explorers of south-eastern Australia and Tasmania. After two successful voyages with Flinders, George Bass, a former ship's surgeon, travelled in an open whaleboat to explore the coast of New South Wales south of Sydney. He left Port Jackson in 1797 and mapped about 500 kilometres of coastline. He then sailed into Western Port. His last journey was to chart the coast of Tasmania with Matthew Flinders.

In the paragraph above, the **main idea** is in **bold**.
Here are notes of the **supporting details**:

- in open whaleboat explored coastline south of Sydney
- mapped 500 kilometres of coastline
- sailed into Western Port
- last journey with Flinders around Tasmania.

Task

Read the paragraph below. **Underline** the **main idea** and **list** the **supporting details**.

First European settlement in Western Australia

In 1827 Captain James Stirling had explored the Swan River area of Western Australia and regarded it as ideal for settlement. He reported to the English government but no one seemed very interested. Soon, however, a gentleman named Thomas Peel decided to set up a group to colonise the area. The group decided that they wanted to settle 10 000 persons in the area. In 1829 Captain Fremantle arrived to take possession of the area. Lieutenant-Governor Stirling arrived soon after and selected the sites of Perth and Fremantle for settlement.

- ____
- ____
  ____
- ____
  ____
- ____
- ____

ACTIVITY 6 Identifying main ideas and supporting details

Read the paragraphs below. **Underline** the **main idea** and **make notes** of the **supporting details**.

1 Trading in the East

The Portuguese, Dutch, English and French traders were keen to establish trading centres in India and the East Indies. The Portuguese were the first to find a sea route to India and quickly established trading centres. The Dutch then began a rich trade in spices from the East Indies. In 1600 the English East India Company was formed. The company set up trading centres in many cities in India, including Surat, Madras, Bombay and Calcutta. The French also joined in and their first settlement was at Pondicherry. The rivalry between the English and French soon led to war.

2 Modern car designers

One of the most famous car designing salons of the last fifty years is the workshop of Nuccio Bertone near Turin in Italy. The Bertone studio has been involved in creating beautiful and stylish shapes for modern cars for many years. Some of his greatest designs can be seen in Lamborghinis, Ferraris and the famous Lancia Stratos. Bertone's earliest creations included the Alfa Romeo Guiletta Sprint and other notable sports cars of the 1950–1980 period. Car companies from many other countries have used Bertone to create appealing designs, for example for the BMW and Volvo. Several English car manufacturers have had designs completed at Bertone's salon.

ACTIVITY 7 Adding supporting detail

1. **Use** the **supporting detail notes** to **complete** the paragraph. The **main idea** is provided for you.

Supporting detail notes
- 1859 — South Australian government offered a reward — first to cross Australia
- Set out 1860 — reached centre of Australia — turned back
- Tried again 1861 — same result
- Third expedition — 1862 — success
- Reached north coast — 24 July

Across Australia

John McDougall Stuart, who first crossed Australia from south to north, was one of Australia's most determined explorers.

2. **Use** the **supporting detail notes** to **complete** the paragraph. The **main idea** is provided for you.

Supporting detail notes
- sleep in trees — centre of their territory
- each day visit waterhole — return to safety of trees
- dawn — out of trees — search for food
- grooming — important part daily routine

Baboons

Various kinds of baboons thrive in many parts of Africa and they all live in troops, usually of between thirty and fifty individuals.

ACTIVITY 8 Adding supporting detail

1 **Use** the **supporting detail notes** to **complete** the paragraph. The **main idea** is provided for you.

Supporting detail notes
- main areas — pastoral zone of Central Queensland — western New South Wales into South Australia
- also western areas — Victoria — south-west of Western Australia
- some areas — wheat and sheep
- many different breeds — 80% merino — others English breeds or crossbreeds
- merinos — very fine wool — quality woollen goods

Wool production

Wool is an important export product for Australia.

2 **Use** the **supporting detail notes** to **complete** the paragraph. The **main idea** is provided for you.

Supporting detail notes
- very still evening — fog rising across the water
- noticed other trawlers — to Ellen Banks — fishing ground
- saw lights flickering — far away port and starboard
- fog closed in — visibility decreased
- suddenly — dead ahead — bright white light — bearing down — trawler

Night watch

As the launch chugged out of the bay Peter stood on the bow, looking ahead.

ACTIVITY 9 Adding supporting detail

A famous navigator, Captain William Bligh, has direct connections to Australia. First, he created an accurate chart of the waters of North Queensland through the Torres Strait. Second, he was appointed governor of New South Wales in 1806.

- Use the Internet to **find information** to complete this activity. A useful website is http://www.questacon.edu.au/html/search.html
- **Add supporting details** to the main ideas listed below to form **four paragraphs**. Include **two** or **three sentences** in your own words for each main idea.

1. William Bligh's life at sea began when he was cabin boy on the HMS *Monmouth*.

2. Bligh's first journey to Tahiti resulted in the famous *Bounty* mutiny.

3. Captain Bligh showed his great leadership and navigation skills after the mutiny.

4. In later years he fought in several naval battles and was a governor.

ACTIVITY 10 Creating paragraphs

Read the notes below and **use** them to **write** a **paragraph** on the topic.

- Use the parts in **bold** to build your **topic sentence** with the main idea.
- Use the **rest** of the notes to provide the **supporting details**.

1

The hawksbill turtle

- **hawksbill turtle — one of several marine turtles — coastal waters of Australia**
- named because of beaklike jaws
- cold blooded — uses sun to warm body
- has attractively marked shell — was hunted widely — now protected
- egg laying — November to February
- female — ashore, coral cays, beaches — northern Australia

2

Earthquakes

- **earthquakes — because — surface of earth — twenty huge plates — move slowly**
- many thousands each year — few cause damage
- large earthquake — maybe 10 000 times energy of first atomic bomb
- greatest disaster — 1556 — Shansi province China — 800 000 killed
- another disaster — 1732 — Calcutta India — 300 000 killed
- main earthquakes — two areas — Circum-Pacific Belt and Alpide Belt

Rules for paragraphs

Paragraphs can be made more precise and effective if the writer uses these three rules:
Rule A Avoid statements that provide information not closely tied to the topic.
Rule B Avoid opinions in factual writing.
Rule C Ensure that facts are not repeated unless they are necessary for special emphasis.
These rules apply particularly to reports and factual recounts.

Task

Read the reports below. **Draw a line** through any sentence that **breaks** any of the three **rules** above. **Indicate** whether the rule broken is **A**, **B** or **C**.

1

Gorillas

Of all the apes in the world the heaviest is the gorilla. They live in the thick equatorial forests and usually live quiet lives. They are not as noisy as chimpanzees and do not groom each other as much. Of all the apes these are the most attractive. Their life in the equatorial forests is very quiet. Many gorillas have been badly treated in circuses over the years.

There are usually about 15–20 gorillas in a troop. An adult male, easily identified because of his larger size and silver-grey back, is the leader of the troop. This male leads the troop in search of food. The gorillas search for food during the day. At night the adult male makes a bed of leaves and twigs low in the trees or on the ground. Many other animals do this as well. The adult male is much larger than any other apes. Gorillas must be the most intelligent of any animal in the animal kingdom.

2

The eye

The eye is just like a tiny but very accurate camera. The pupil of the eye is like the aperture of a camera. Good eyesight is very important for driving at night. The pupil of the eye can enlarge in dim conditions to let more light enter the eye. The lens and the cornea make up a focusing team that is similar to a camera lens. The aperture of a camera is very similar to the pupil of the eye. The retina operates in much the same way as the film of a camera.

The light comes into the eye from many different points. When the beams of light reach the surface of the cornea they become bent, or refracted. It is possible to have cornea transplants these days. The light passes through the cornea and is focused on the retina. Some people have trouble with tears in the retina. The retina is much the same as the film in a camera. The focusing of these points of light on the retina creates a tiny image of the scene.

Paragraphs in dialogue

In a narrative that includes a conversation, **each speaker**'s comments **make up** a **single paragraph**.

Example

Paragraph 1 'What are you doing?' asked Sharnie. 'I thought I told you to collect all the items and place them in the blue containers.'

Paragraph 2 'That's what I'm doing', answered Emily, 'but it's taking a lot longer than I thought'.

Paragraph 3 'Well, hurry and finish so that we can both go to the movies', said Sharnie in an exasperated tone.

Task

- **Read** the following pieces of dialogue.
- **Underline** the **first word** of each paragraph.
- **Insert quotation marks** and **punctuation** where necessary.

1. Quickly close the door behind you whispered Mary urgently as she moved past the table

   what on earth for asked Toni in a puzzled tone and she walked towards the open door

   I just heard someone outside or at least I'm pretty sure I did replied Mary

   Oh, you are just imagining things again answered Toni with a smile on her face.

2. I'm afraid I lost my favourite Labrador dog a few days ago said Sam in a sorrowful tone

   Well said Sarah why don't you put up notices around the area or an advertisement in the newspaper

   Probably wouldn't do much good answered Sam I never did get around to teaching him to read

3. That new driving instructor you hired for me is terrible Louise said in a dejected tone

   Why do you say that asked her husband Tim surprised by his wife's comment

   Well today he nearly killed me three times with his silly advice when I was driving replied Louise

   Oh come on dear the husband replied why don't we give him one more chance

7 Setting a scene

In this chapter you will learn how to **add details** to your writing so that the reader can easily visualise the scene you have in mind. A piece of writing is more interesting when details such as **specific names**, **expressive adjectives** and **expressive verbs** are added. Words or phrases indicating **time** and **place** also help provide a clearer scene.

Example

- The boy ran over.
- Grant, the tall, dark-haired boy from next door rushed over
  (expressive adjective) (expressive verb)
  to the gleaming red Porsche a few minutes ago.
  (place) (time)

Visualising the scene

Before setting a scene for a reader, the writer must have a clear idea of the scene. The writer must first **visualise** the **scene**.

Start with a few **ideas**.

ski boat — skier — sketch of water

Adding details

The first ideas then have to be brought into focus by **adding details**. These questions would be useful to help you add detail:

- Where is the stretch of water?
- How many people are involved?
- What is the weather like?
- What kind of boat is being used?

The writer can then use her responses to these questions to set an interesting scene.

It was a beautifully clear day at Lake Tinaroo. The surface of the lake was like a mirror as the sun glistened on the surface. Suddenly from the western side a tall fair-haired skier appeared out of the water. Towing the skier was a dark green speedboat called *Exterminator*. On the boat the blonde female driver gunned the engine towards the centre of the lake. Sitting behind her, another woman acted as observer.

ACTIVITY 1 Adding details

- **Consider** the first ideas.
- **Use** the **picture** to answer the questions and to provide details to set the scene.
- **Write** a paragraph describing the scene.

1. **First ideas:** ship in harbour — unloading

Questions:

- What type of ship is it?
- Where is the harbour?
- What is being unloaded?
- What is being taken away on horse drawn wagons?
- What type of cargo has been stacked on the wharf?

2. **First ideas:** swimming pool — swimming and fun

Questions:

- Where is the pool?
- Which people are swimming laps of the pool?
- Which adult is about to dive into the pool?
- What is the small boy doing?
- Who is just paying to come into the pool area?

Using general and specific names

Using **specific names** instead of general names helps the reader to have the **clearest picture** of a scene.

Example

The two words in **bold** in this sentence are general names:

- The **animal** was eating its **food**.

To set the scene more clearly, the writer could have used specific names, as in these examples:

- The **lion** was eating the **meat**.
- The **cat** was eating the **fish**.
- The **elephant** was eating the **green fodder**.
- The **eagle** was eating the **small creature**.
- The **youth** was eating the **hamburger**.

Task

1 **Circle** the **word** in each set of three that would give the reader the **clearest picture** of the scene.

a ocean, water, lake

b building, cathedral, structure

c garment, skirt, clothing

d invention, machinery, photocopier

e game, competition, volleyball

f person, warder, official

g plant, thistle, weed

h music, song, blues

2 **Write specific nouns** to replace the general nouns in **bold** in these sentences.

a The teenagers were canoeing on the **water**. ______________________

b The **vehicle** was damaged in the accident. ______________________

c He put the **meat** on the barbecue. ______________________

d Much of the **food** had been stored away. ______________________

e The **wood** was placed near the outside wall. ______________________

f Many **things** had been scattered about. ______________________

g Sharon can play that **instrument** really well. ______________________

h Look at the **items** on the back seat. ______________________

i Have you emptied the **container** yet? ______________________

j The **fuel** for the machine was in the shed. ______________________

k The scuffling of the **animal** disturbed them. ______________________

ACTIVITY 2 Adding details and specific names

- **Consider** the first ideas.
- **Use** the **picture** to answer the questions.
- **Write** a **paragraph**, using the answers and specific names to set the scenes.

1 **First ideas:** Jack and Laura Ralston's farm — black pony — Tewala, Arabian mare — Antares

Questions:

- Where is the owner's house?
- What is Jack working on?
- Where are the two horses?
- What are their names?
- What are they doing?
- What type of building is close to the horses?
- What would be kept in the building?

2 **First ideas:** Carol and Mike Lawson at beach with boy, Adam, and toddler, Marcus

Questions:

- What type of day is it?
- What are the parents doing?
- What is Adam playing with?
- What is Marcus doing?
- What are other children playing?
- Which building overlooks the beach?

ACTIVITY 3 Using specific names

Read each paragraph below. **Replace** the general names in **bold** with **specific names** to give a clearer picture of the scene.

1 All the **adults** (____________________) went with the **children** (____________________) out into the farmland. Here they saw many **citrus** (____________________) trees growing well in the deep soil. Nearby, many huge gardens of **vegetables** (____________________) were almost ready for harvesting. One **worker** (____________________) noticed that **something** (____________________) was eating the leaves of some of the plants. They all tried to find the **creature** (____________________) that was doing the damage.

2 The **dog** (____________________) and the **cat** (____________________) had been on the lawn. It seemed as if they had been chasing the **insects** (____________________) under the **fruit** (____________________) trees. Soon they scampered over to the **building** (____________________) that housed the **boat** (____________________), which belonged to the **people** (____________________).

3 Our **relatives** (____________________) visited us some **time** (____________________) ago. They always visited us to play **games** (____________________) in the rough country near our home. It was important to wear sturdy **footwear** (____________________). We had built a small **shelter** (____________________). Sometimes **toys** (____________________) were left there for weeks. At one **place** (____________________) nearby was the perfect place for playing **ballgames** (____________________).

4 The **carnivore** (____________________) came out of the **place** (____________________). It was clear that it had a wounded **limb** (____________________). A small **mammal** (____________________) crossed its path but it made no attempt to chase it. The **people** (____________________) working in the **place** (____________________) hoped to be able to tranquillise the injured animal. One **worker** (____________________) used a **weapon** (____________________) to shoot a dart into the creature. Before long they were able to treat the injured animal.

Adding adjectives

Setting a scene involves bringing **first ideas into focus** by using **specific names**. To give an even clearer picture of the scene, **describing words** can be used.

Example

- **The kitten was in the basket.**

The scene is much clearer if we add some adjectives or describing words.

The <u>tiny</u>, <u>silver-grey</u> kitten was in the <u>yellow</u> basket.

- **The animal bounded out of the thicket.**

The scene is much clearer if we use specific names and describing words.

The <u>fierce lion</u> bounded out of the <u>dense</u> thicket.

Task

1 **Rewrite** the sentences, providing clearer scenes by **adding describing words** to the words in **bold**.

a The **window** was in the **shed**. ______

b His **brother** had climbed the **tree**. ______

c The **man** opened the **box**. ______

d The **cake** was placed on the **table**. ______

e The **coins** were on the **counter**. ______

2 **Rewrite** the sentences, providing clearer scenes by **using specific names** and **adding describing words** for the words in **bold**.

a The **vehicle** travelled along the **road**. ______

b **He** followed the **dog**. ______

c The **creek** flowed through the **valley**. ______

d The **bird** flew to the **tree**. ______

e On the **desk** was a **dish**. ______

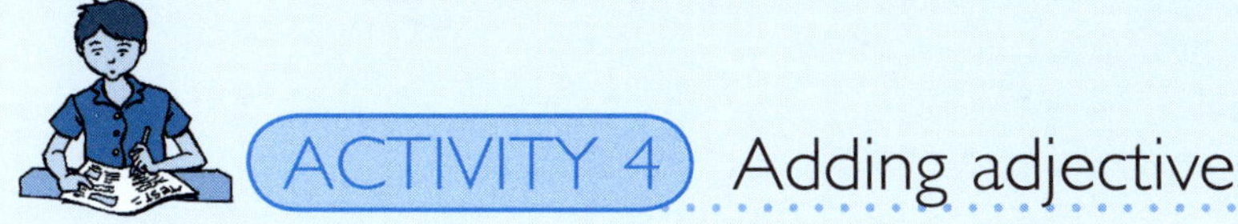

ACTIVITY 4 Adding adjectives

1 **Read** the following pairs of sentences. One sentence of each pair uses specific names and suitable describing words. **Tick** (✓) the box after this sentence. **Circle** the **specific names** and **describing words**.

a The forest in the valley was shrouded in mist. ☐
The most sheltered forest in Erin Valley was shrouded in fine mist. ☐

b The grey-haired old man was chopping the huge pile of dry wood. ☐
The old man was chopping the pile of wood. ☐

c The young pony galloped across the yard. ☐
The spirited young Arabian pony galloped across the wide training yard. ☐

d The speeding sedan had been repaired at the workshop. ☐
The speeding yellow Ford had been repaired at the modern, well-equipped workshop. ☐

e They took a short trip to the nearest zoo. ☐
The excited family took a short trip to the newly opened zoo. ☐

f Many small kittens played happily in the basket. ☐
Many small Persian kittens played happily in the fur-lined basket. ☐

g All along the busy street vehicles travelled quickly. ☐
All along the crowded, busy street the tiny mopeds travelled quickly. ☐

h The tall steel building shone brightly in the early morning sun. ☐
The tall building shone brightly in the sun. ☐

i Many of the colourful lorikeets in the area rested in the tall, stately pines. ☐
Many of the birds in the area rested in the tall trees. ☐

2 **Add** at least **two** suitable **describing words** and **specific names** to each sentence to set a clearer scene.

a He and his sister went to the event.

____

____

b The actor waited at the door to the stage.

____

____

c The boy's cousins enjoyed the film.

____

____

d The ship was sailing through the strait.

____

e The toy was used to amuse the children.

____

f The fruits and vegetables were collected by them.

____

Using expressive verbs

Using **expressive verbs** in your writing is another way you can make the scene clearer for the reader.

Examples

- The girl **went** down the road.
- The girl **raced** down the road.
- The girl **trudged** down the road.

- The verbs in bold help set the scene. In the first sentence the verb *went* does not give a clear indication of how the girl travelled. She could have walked, run, ridden a bike or gone by car.
- The second and third sentences set the scene more clearly. The verbs *raced* and *trudged* indicate exactly how she travelled.
- The verbs *raced* and *trudged* are much more expressive than the verb *went*.

Here are some expressive verb alternatives for common verbs.

move	budge	stir	proceed	shift	advance	trudge		
run	dart	sprint	jog	dash	trot	scamper	scurry	
hit	strike	knock	jab	punch	smack	slap	thrash	smite
jeer	deride	mock	revile	sneer	taunt	ridicule		
get	obtain	acquire	procure	fetch	attain	achieve	gain	
give	present	donate	grant	award	contribute	distribute		

Task

Select the most suitable **expressive verb** from the box above to **replace** the word in **bold**.

1. The explorers will (**move**) ____________________ across the steep mountainous region.
2. The frightened rabbit will (**run**) ____________________ back into its burrow.
3. They will (**hit**) ____________________ each of the rugs several times to remove dust particles.
4. It was particularly rude of him to (**jeer at**) ____________________ the work of the other students.
5. The author tried to (**get**) ____________________ his goal of completing three books this year.
6. The president will (**give**) ____________________ the student the winner's prize.

ACTIVITY 5 Using expressive verbs

1. **Circle** the **verb** in the brackets that **more clearly** sets the scene.
   - a The girl (walked, skipped) happily down the path.
   - b She (took, snatched) the ball from her brother.
   - c The miner (hit, struck) the side of the machine heavily.
   - d They all (went, stomped) off into the tent.
   - e The angry woman was (shaking, holding) the wooden stake.
   - f The furious tiger was (coming, rushing) towards the villagers.
   - g Many of the coins had (tumbled, fallen) from the purse.
   - h Caught in the act, the burglar (got, jumped) to his feet.

2. **Choose** an **expressive verb** from the box to help set the scene in each sentence.

sneaked	crouched	hurled	smashed	crashed
glared	eased	lingered	snarled	

   - a The timid creature ____________________ in the shade of the wall.
   - b The customer ____________________ angrily at the shop attendant.
   - c The injured woman was ____________________ out of the damaged vehicle by the paramedics.
   - d All the fans ____________________ around the stage door long after the concert was over.
   - e The wild beast ____________________ angrily as it leapt away.
   - f The runaway truck ____________________ through the trees near the creek.
   - g The athlete ____________________ the javelin across the oval with ease.
   - h The thief ____________________ through the kitchen and into the hallway.
   - i The skilled batsman ____________________ the ball over the grandstand.

3. **Replace** the words in **bold** with more **expressive verbs**.

   The huge truck was **going** (____________________) down the highway. As it **ran** (____________________) up the steep hill into town the engine was working hard. By the time it **got to** (____________________) the top the truck had slowed to a crawl. Soon it **got to** (____________________) the downhill slope out of town. The bridge was not far away. As the driver **put on** (____________________) the brakes he knew they had gone. The huge truck **hit** (____________________) the bridge railings and **went** (____________________) into the river. Fortunately, the driver was able to **get out of** (____________________) the sinking vehicle.

4. **Write** suitable **expressive verbs** to **match** these common verbs.
   - a walk: ____
   - b speak: ____
   - c eat: ____

Using expressive verbs

Verbs show the **actions** of the **characters** in a narrative. Expressive verbs help you to give a **clear picture**.

Note the difference in these sets of sentences. The different verbs give a different picture of the action.

Examples

- The boy **stumbled** wearily into the room.
- The boy **ran** into the room.
- The boy **skipped** happily into the room.

- The old car **spluttered** along the driveway.
- The speeding vehicle **careered** off the road.
- The sports car **roared** around the track.

Task

1 **Choose** an **expressive verb** from the box for each sentence to give a clearer picture of the action.

scrambled	spurred	whistled	blurted	slammed
charged	ambled	nudged	trotted	hopped

a The tired old man ______________________ along the path.
b The shrieking wind ______________________ through the rigging of the ship.
c The pony ________________ across the paddock to its mother.
d The climber __________________ up the steep slope with ease.
e The rider ______________________ her horse around the track to the finish line.
f The speeding truck ______________ into the edge of the bridge.
g The ferocious lion _____________________ rapidly towards the intruders.
h The German shepherd gently __________________ the little pup along the path.
i The tiny wallaby quickly ____________________ back into its mother's pouch at any sign of danger.
j The child was so anxious he ____________________ out the answer instantly.

2 **Choose** an **expressive phrase** from the box to **complete** the sentences.

grumbled quietly	sobbed uncontrollably	interrupted rudely	rumbled loudly
struggled wearily	waddled awkwardly	advanced carefully	trotted proudly

a The unhappy girl ____.
b The tall, arrogant stranger ______________________________________.
c The disappointed child ____.
d All the runners ____.
e The thunder in the east ____.
f The prize-winning Arab pony ____________________________________.
g The toddler ____.
h The attacking soldiers ____.

Adding time and place

In order to arouse the reader's interest, a **word picture** has to cover three points:

- **characters**
- **actions**
- **setting**.

The **setting** includes the **time** and **place**. The setting for a ghost story may be a haunted house, while the setting for a travel adventure may be a rugged mountainous area. Choosing the appropriate setting for a narrative is easy, but to create an accurate word picture of the setting, words and phrases indicating time and place are needed, in addition to descriptive words and phrases.

In the example below, the words in **bold** indicate **time** and **place**. Also note the **descriptive sections**, which provide a clearer word picture of the setting.

Example

It was after five when Jan and Jana arrived at the building. **On the opposite side of the street** was a derelict warehouse. The hundreds of windows **high up on the front wall** were a grimy brown and the blistered flaking paint showed years of neglect. **Toward the southern end** was a huge roller door with chains and padlocks. It did not seem possible that anyone had lived or worked there **for many years**. In silence the two private investigators waited **in their vehicle as darkness fell**. Soon the building was bathed in soft moonlight.

Read the paragraph below and then read the following one, which sets the scene more clearly.

Example

We were in the country. We decided to see if we could find the early settlers' huts. After some time we managed to find one of them. We wanted to find out if there were any things left in the hut. When we went inside we noticed several broken pieces of furniture and the floor strewn with rubbish.

We were **at our Uncle George's place** in the country **last summer**. **One clear day** Sharnia and I decided to look for the early settlers' huts. Uncle George had mentioned them **many times**. **The previous night**, as we sat **by the fireplace**, he had mentioned them again. **Early in the morning** we set out for **the southern boundary**, **about three kilometres away**. **Around mid-morning** we glimpsed the broken-down remains of one of the huts. **Within half an hour** we reached the crumbling hut **on the edge of an overgrown garden**. Peering **into the gloomy interior** we noticed several broken pieces of furniture lying **in the midst of** a pile of mouldy rubbish.

ACTIVITY 6 Adding time and place

1. **Read** the pairs of settings below. **Tick** (✓) the box for the one that you think gives the clearer word picture of the setting. **Underline time** and **place** words and phrases that help provide the clearer word picture.

   a i They were playing inside the shed. It had rained for some time and the path was now under water. They hurried along the edge to stack the equipment by the doorway. ☐

   ii They had been playing for almost an hour inside the new shed. For several hours rain had been falling and the narrow path was covered with water. They hurried along the side of the building to stack their game equipment in the rows of boxes near the doorway. ☐

   b i Soon the group had entered the cave. In the stillness they could hear the water trickling down the rocks near the entrance. With torches lighting the way, the group began the perilous climb down the narrow passageway to the rock pools below. ☐

   ii Within a few minutes the group had entered the narrow cave. In the stillness they could just hear the bubbling sound of water softly cascading down the rock face within metres of the entrance. Using torches, the group lit their path as they began the dangerous descent of the narrow, moss-covered passageway, which snaked down to the silent rock pools below. ☐

2. **Read** this set of sentences and then **rewrite** them, **adding time** and **place phrases** to set the scene more clearly.

   The cousins scrambled up the cliff. They stared at the entrance of a cave. They heard the muffled sound of a creature. Curious, they entered the cave to locate the animal.

ACTIVITY 7 Adding time and place

1 **Read** these outlines. **Add time** and **place** words and phrases. Include **descriptive aspects**.

a (time) ______________________ several of the workers began moving the rubble from the building site. Broken bricks, stones and (descriptive) ______________________ littered the area. The actual site was located (place) ______________________ and had been used as a dump for several years. (time) ______________________ the largest items had been removed. These had been taken to (place) ______________________ ______________ by (descriptive) ______________________ trucks.

b (time) ______________________ and the heat beat down mercilessly. The travellers were in the (place) ______________________ and the huge boulder-strewn plateau was a terrible obstacle to the weary group. (time) ______________________ __________ the lack of water created additional hardship. (time) ______________________ ______________ they had reached the midpoint of the (descriptive) ______________________ ______________ region. Overcome with weariness, they rested (place) ______________________ ______________ (time) ______________________. Setting out again, they realised that they had sufficient food for only the next three days.

2 **Create** a **word picture** by using descriptive words, and time and place words and phrases, from this outline.

> forced landing — light aircraft — four passengers plus pilot — engine problems — landed on disused strip — far west New South Wales — minor injuries — isolated area

ACTIVITY 8 Adding time and place

1. **Read** the paragraph below. **Rewrite** it, **adding** phrases and groups of words **to indicate time** and **place**. **Underline** your additions.

> The two youngsters, Alan and Marcia, decided to set out. Their boat moved quickly across the water. Soon they reached the reef. They checked their diving gear, masks, flippers and spear guns. Then Marcia decided to dive in first. Alan watched as she entered the water.

2. **Read** the outline notes below. **Rewrite** them as **sentences**, including phrases and groups of words to **indicate time** and **place**.

> sun — brightly — team — athletes — stadium.
> colourful spectacle — marched — track.
> after march — competitors lined up — centre — stadium.
> speech delivered — Olympic Torch — into arena.
> choir sang Olympic hymn — huge cheer.

ACTIVITY 9 Setting a scene

In this chapter you have focused on how to write clearer scenes by:

- adding **details**
- using **expressive verbs**
- using **specific names**
- using phrases **indicating time** and **place**
- adding **describing words**.

Here are the **first ideas** of a writer.

Three young people — log cabin — horse riding — nearby peak
rough slopes — difficulties — reach — outlook

1. **Think about** this scene and **complete** the **table**.

Extra details	Specific names	Describing words	Expressive verbs	Time and place phrases

2. **Write six** to **eight sentences** built on the first ideas. **Use** the words and phrases from the table.

ACTIVITY 10 Setting a scene

Consider the **five points** raised in this chapter:

- adding **details**
- using **expressive verbs**
- using **specific names**
- using phrases **indicating time** and **place**
- adding **describing words**.

1 **Write six** to **eight sentences** built on the first ideas outlined in the box.

school group — excursion — bus trip — sunny day — heavy traffic — museum — special display

2 **Write six** to **eight sentences** built on the first ideas outlined in the box.

trail bike — clear day — four riders — left after breakfast — unloaded bikes — winding tracks — jumps — hours of fun

8 Creating word pictures

In this chapter you will learn how to create **word pictures** to help the reader visualise the **scene**. There are a number of ways to make these pictures **more vivid**.

Appeal to the five senses

To create a descriptive **word picture** a writer has to **appeal** to the **senses** of the reader. The word picture has to include words that the reader will associate with the five senses:

- **sight**
- **sound**
- **smell**
- **taste**
- **touch**.

Examples

Sight: They looked across the **sandy brown desert country**.

Sound: The angry lion **growled fiercely** at the intruders.

Smell: The **tantalising odour of freshly baked bread** wafted through the building.

Taste: The **delicious sweetness** of the liquid was a great enjoyment.

Touch: The cat purred as it settled itself into the **warm fur-lined** basket.

Include feelings and emotions

In addition to the five senses, **feelings** and **emotions** can be expressed by words and phrases. Here are some examples.

anger	love	affection	boredom	fright
pride	agony	happiness	disappointment	

Use similes and metaphors

Similes and metaphors are frequently used to create word pictures.

Similes usually start with *like* or *as* and two things are compared.

Example

- His **hands** were <u>as</u> cold as **ice**.

Metaphors are written in a different way. Instead of comparing two things, a metaphor describes one of the items as something else.

Example

- The **aircraft** <u>was</u> a **silver bird** streaking across the sky.

Describe people's appearance

When writers describe people, they create word pictures by giving **details** of their **appearance**: height, build, eyes, hair, skin, clothing, footwear, distinguishing marks, expressions, gestures and general attitude. These details allow the writer to create people who can be visualised easily by the reader.

Appealing to the senses

Word pictures use words that appeal to the **senses** of the reader.

The five senses

sight sound smell touch taste

Task

1. **Which** of the **five senses** shown above did the writer use to create the descriptive word picture in **bold**? **Write** the answer on the line.

   a The **harsh rat-tat-tat beat** of the drum could be heard some distance away. ____________

   b A **smoky-bacon aroma** rose from the pot on the stove. ____________

   c The **dark shadowy valley** filled them with dread. ____________

   d She enjoyed the meal with a **variety of spicy flavours**. ____________

   e The **silky-soft material** was used to create attractive sportswear. ____________

   f **Warbling sweetly** in the bushes were several native birds. ____________

   g **Large, unusually shaped trees** dotted the edge of the forest. ____________

2. **Add** suitable words to **create** a descriptive word picture.

   a The ____________ swamp was the home of many alligators.

   b The ____________ building was one that tourists often visited.

   c All of the ____________ art works were kept under strict security.

3. **Study** the picture below. **Create three sentences** using words that refer to any of the five senses.

   - **Sentence 1**: coffee
   - **Sentence 2**: food
   - **Sentence 3**: music

ACTIVITY 1 Appealing to the senses

Study the pictures below. **Create descriptive word pictures** of **four** or **five sentences**, using words referring to the **five senses**. **Use** some of the **clue words** in the box.

1

Clues

- acrobatic rider
- flashily dressed ringmaster
- vocal crowd
- decorated horse
- brightly coloured costume
- whip cracking

2

Clues

- ragged and torn clothing
- buzzing of insects
- well-worn path
- gaudy plumage of tropical birds
- cool mist and rain
- moist smell of decaying leaf litter

ACTIVITY 2 Appealing to the senses

1. **Read** each pair of sentences. One sentence will **appeal more strongly** to the **senses**. **Circle** it and **write** which of the five senses the writer used.
   - a i These particular chocolates are very appetising.
     ii Rich dark chocolate with sultanas is almost irresistible. ____________
   - b i A common smell arose from the pot on the stove.
     ii They noticed the sticky sweet aroma of the pudding. ____________
   - c i The huge church bells tolled early in the day.
     ii The mournful note of the bell echoed across the valley. ____________
   - d i There is a very interesting view across the canyon.
     ii The vision of distant ranges and canyons was enchanting. ____________
   - e i The kitten enjoyed the soft caress of the little girl.
     ii The child was stroking the cat by the fire. ____________
   - f i She caught a vivid glimpse of the city through the lightning strikes.
     ii The image of the town could be seen clearly. ____________

2. **Expand** these sentences by **adding** words that appeal to the **sense** in brackets to describe each word in **bold**.
   - a The **image** was particularly attractive. (sight)
   - b The **noise** could be heard across the valley. (sound)
   - c The **fragrance** drifted slowly on the wind. (smell)
   - d The **flavour** was very popular. (taste)
   - e The **contact** was very painful. (touch)
   - f The **mountain** rose in the distance. (sight)
   - g The **sound** of the guns could be heard. (sound)
   - h The **toast** was placed on the shelf. (smell)

ACTIVITY 3 Appealing to the senses

1 To create a vivid description a writer must mainly appeal to the sense of sight. **Read** the paragraph below. **Underline** those sections that appeal to the **sense** of **sight**.

The sleek, four-masted sailing vessel hove to some distance from the island and the longboat was lowered. Nearing the small, densely forested island—gleaming in the first rays of the tropical sun—the sailors saw smoke snaking from a campfire some distance inland. Fearing that the island might be inhabited by hostile forces, they returned to the ship. Soon the longboat set off again, well armed this time, to land on the small golden stretch of beach where palm trees stretched forward towards the white-tipped swells. The wary sailors were closely examining the undergrowth when suddenly a wild figure appeared. Clad in ragged clothes of goatskin and with long matted hair and beard, the creature rushed towards the sailors.

2 **Add** sections that appeal to the **sense** of **sight** to this description. The illustration will help you.

The frame was ____

and ____.

On the right-hand side ____________________________________. The painting was of ____________________________, which were shading a ________________

________________. On the right-hand side of the pool was ______________________________

who was wearing ______________________________________ and had a

______________________________________ draped across his shoulders. The hills in the background were ______________________________, showing that several bushfires had been through the area.

Including feelings and emotions

Descriptive words and **phrases** can be used to express **feelings** and **emotions**. These are some of the feelings and emotions that can be shown in your writing.

anger	love	affection	boredom	fright
pride	agony	happiness	disappointment	

Task

Identify which of the **feelings** in the box are shown in these paragraphs.

1. It was another long, dreary day. Sharon knew it straight away. Nowhere to go. Nothing to do. Just another miserable overcast day and hours to put in until bedtime. ______________
2. Jack looked at the broken toy. It had shattered into pieces on the kitchen floor. His pleasure in the new toy was gone. A feeling of sadness came over him as he began collecting the tiny pieces. ______________
3. Simba, his favourite Abyssinian cat, bounded towards him. With a strange little cry it jumped on his lap. Hedley watched as Simba curled up and purred contentedly. Hedley began stroking his tiny companion while smiling with fondness at his delightful friend. ______________
4. What a wonderful present! Ellen was so pleased. The instrument her parents had bought was just what she wanted. Now her dream of becoming a member of the local music group was a possibility. She could hardly stop smiling to herself as she removed the shiny golden saxophone from the strong vinyl-covered case. ______________
5. It was not working again. Jason looked carefully at the CD player, his temper beginning to rise. He had taken the player to be repaired and it was still quite useless. His exasperation and displeasure could be seen in every movement. Suddenly, with a shout of fury, he hurled the player through the open window. ______________
6. Toni waited patiently in the car park. She had been there for two hours waiting for her friends to arrive. The dark shadows were lengthening and a fresh, cold breeze was picking up. She shivered as the cold seeped into her light clothing. Suddenly she was aware of a slight thudding sound behind her. Cautiously she looked around. An expression of dismay crossed her face as a huge dog growled at her. ______________
7. The final lap was about to begin. Chris was in third place but well placed to finish well. He heard the bell. Here was his chance. In the last event he had had to settle for second place but he felt this time he would win. He was delighted with his place at this stage and reminded himself of the honours he would receive for winning. He surged forward, his strong legs carrying him to the lead, and to his delight he stayed there to the finish. His satisfaction with his effort as he crossed the tape was plain to see. ______________
8. The throbbing pain struck him just before noon. Soon it had passed to his lower jaw and each breath brought on spasms of pain. The cold air seemed to increase the discomfort and it was all he could do to avoid groaning in misery as the pain reached new, extreme levels. ______________

ACTIVITY 4 Including feelings and emotions

Use descriptive words and **phrases** to create word pictures showing the **feelings** listed. Use the scene provided and limit your response to **three** or **four sentences**.

1. **Feeling:** fright. **Scene:** someone about to enter creek and crocodile sleeping near log close to water

2. **Feeling:** happiness. **Scene:** unwrapping birthday presents on carpet in lounge room

3. **Feeling:** affection. **Scene:** welcoming pet dog home after visit to vet for treatment

4. **Feeling:** disappointment. **Scene:** watching heavy rain begin to fall as trip to theme park is cancelled

Using similes and metaphors

Similes and metaphors are frequently used to appeal to the senses.

- **Similes** usually start with *like* or *as* and two things are **compared**:
  The **baby rabbit** was like a whitish **ball** of cotton wool.
- **Metaphors** are written in a different way. Instead of comparing two things, a metaphor describes one of the items **as something else**:
  The **track** was a dusty **ribbon** through the sparse forest.

Note: similes and metaphors can help to create word pictures but they should be used sparingly.

Task

1. **Underline** the **similes** in these sentences.
   - a The young sprinter was as swift as a gazelle.
   - b The shirt that he wore was as white as snow.
   - c A sound like thunder echoed across the valley.
   - d The active child was as playful as a kitten.
   - e After the long day he was as hungry as a lion.
   - f A large cloud like tufts of golden wool could be seen as the sun rose.

2. **Circle** the **metaphors** in these sentences.
   - a The cat was a delightful bundle of excitement.
   - b Many of the old trees were ghostly shapes on the ridge.
   - c The sailing vessel was a silver galleon bathed in the moonlight.
   - d The sun shining through the hole was a golden shaft of light.
   - e Some of the mountains were jagged pyramids of shining rock.
   - f The decorations were a writhing mass of colour and movement.

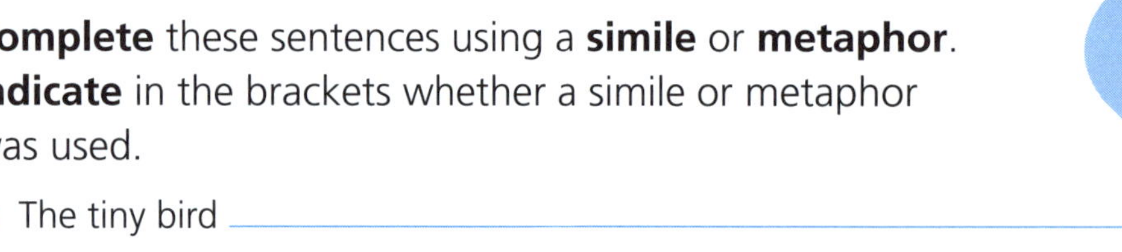

3. **Complete** these sentences using a **simile** or **metaphor**. **Indicate** in the brackets whether a simile or metaphor was used.

   - a The tiny bird ______________________________ (__________)
   - b The large white tent ______________________________ (__________)
   - c Some of the art works ______________________________ (__________)
   - d My young cousin ______________________________ (__________)
   - e The fighter aircraft ______________________________ (__________)

Creating real people—describing appearance

When you write **characters** into a story, it is important to give the reader a **clear picture**. To do this you have to note certain details:

- height
- build
- eyes
- hair
- skin
- clothing
- footwear
- distinguishing marks.

In the example below, the descriptive details are shown in **bold**.

Example

Jack Ralston stood by the fence waiting for us. He was **over two metres in height, thin and agile looking**. **Dark brown eyes** peered out from under a **mass of thick, black, curly hair**. It was obvious that his skin had been **tanned by the hot tropical sun**. **Strange tattoos** were visible on his **thin, sinewy arms**. Wearing a pair of **ragged brown shorts and a faded red shirt**, he smiled broadly at us as we approached.

Sometimes it is not necessary to include all the details listed above. Often it is best to leave some out and **concentrate on those details** that make the **person different** from other people.

Task

Below are a number of characters and some descriptive details.
Circle the **two descriptive details** you would be most likely to use for the character.

1. newborn baby:
   - a tiny, delicate fingers
   - b long, powerful legs
   - c soft, silken hair
   - d large, muscular arms
2. lion cub:
   - a fluffy, golden paws
   - b bright, playful eyes
   - c deep, booming roar
   - d wild, yellow mane
3. old sailor:
   - a suntanned, muscular arms
   - b small, narrow shoulders
   - c soft, wispy hair
   - d weather-beaten, lined face
4. long-distance runner:
   - a lean, powerful legs
   - b large, well-built frame
   - c smooth running action
   - d carefully groomed appearance
5. female dancer:
   - a long, tied-back golden hair
   - b fierce black eyes
   - c nervous, strained features
   - d slim, agile body
6. weight-lifter:
   - a huge, bulging biceps
   - b delicately groomed hair
   - c thin, scrawny legs
   - d solid, muscular body

Creating real people—expressions and attitudes

As well as the details of their appearance, it can be useful when **describing characters** to include their **expressions**, **gestures** and **general attitude**.

In the example below, the descriptive details are shown in **bold**. They include the character's expressions and gestures as well as his physical appearance.

Example

The old artist had a **rough face** with **reddish-brown skin**. His **lower lip jutted out** below his top lip. He was dressed in a **light brown, threadbare robe**. His nose was **turned up slightly at the end** and an **expression of anger** flooded across his face. His eyes were **large and dark** and his cheeks showed **dark hollows** on either side of his face. His arms **moved wildly** as he criticised the work. His feelings of **rage and disappointment** were clearly visible.

Read the example below. Note how descriptive details such as height, build, eyes, hair, skin, clothing, footwear, distinguishing marks, expressions, gestures and general attitude have been used to complete the description.

The ranger

Paula Ellis was a ranger with the National Parks and Wildlife Service. At about thirty years of age she had had a great deal of experience in the field. She stood by her vehicle eager to set out. About average in height, her fitness for the task was evident in her slim, muscular body. Despite the years of exposure to the sun her complexion was clear with a pinkish skin tone on her oval-shaped face. Her deep, piercing blue eyes sparkled with life and a wide grin spread across her face as we approached. She indicated with her right hand that we should climb on to the vehicle. With a toss of her dark ponytail she took the driver's seat. With an enthusiastic greeting to all of us she started the engine and we moved off on the trip to the Cape.

Task

Read the sentences below. **Tick** (✓) the sentence in each pair that provides a **clearer word picture**.

1. a The girl was a tall, fair-haired netball player.
   b The tall, athletic girl wore the bold red netball outfit.
2. a The man had a big hat, a grey coat and leather boots.
   b The man had a black cowboy hat, a long, woven grey coat and tanned boots.
3. a Her neatly combed fair hair glistened in the rays of brilliant sunshine.
   b She wore her neat fair hair pulled back and it shone in the sun.
4. a Over in the corner was a small ginger kitten.
   b In a dark and damp corner of the room was a tiny, ginger kitten.
5. a Jason, the pilot, was dressed immaculately in a black lounge suit with pearl buttons.
   b The pilot, Jason, had dressed in a black suit with some pearl buttons.

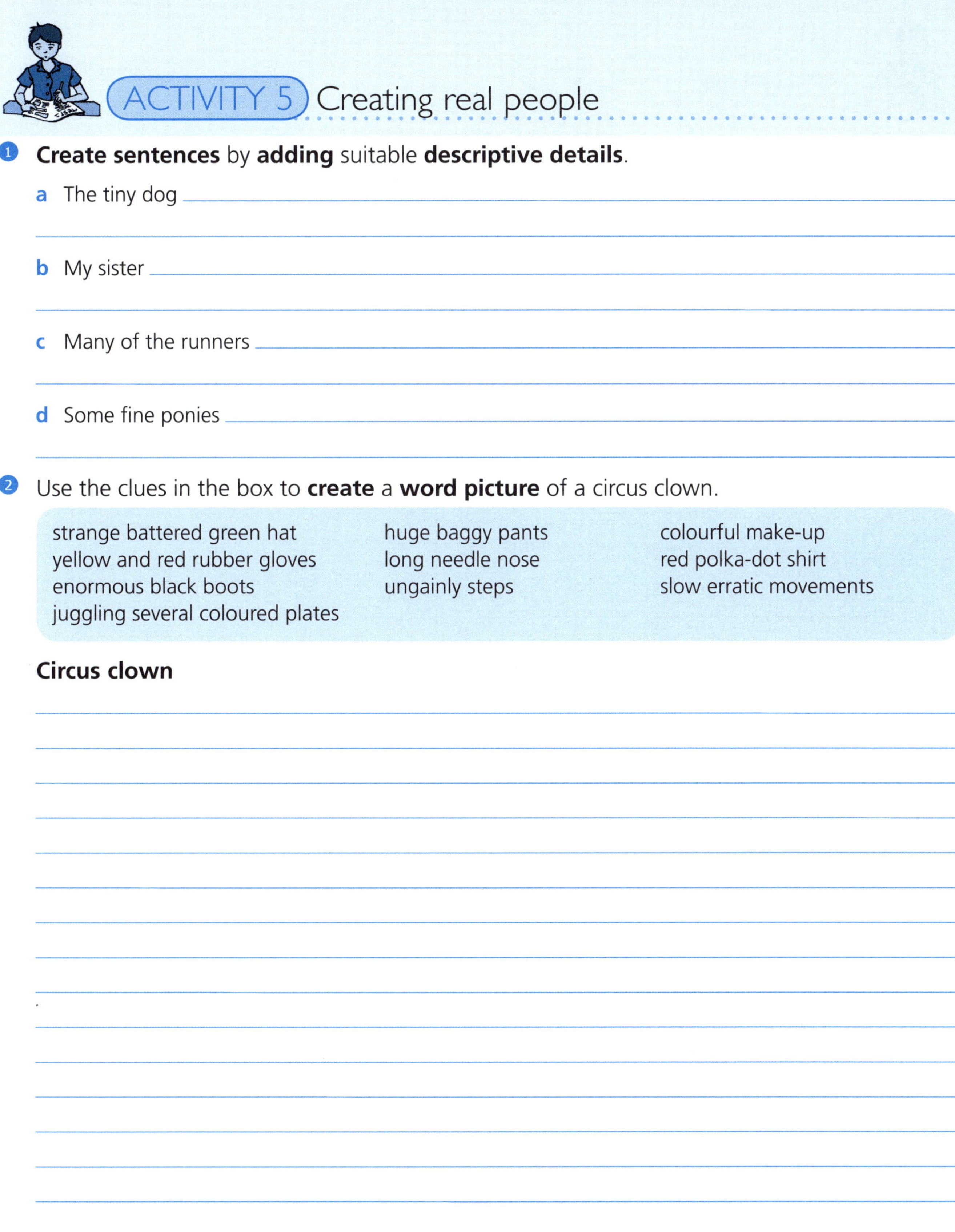

ACTIVITY 5 Creating real people

1 **Create sentences** by **adding** suitable **descriptive details**.

a The tiny dog ______

b My sister ______

c Many of the runners ______

d Some fine ponies ______

2 Use the clues in the box to **create** a **word picture** of a circus clown.

strange battered green hat
yellow and red rubber gloves
enormous black boots
juggling several coloured plates
huge baggy pants
long needle nose
ungainly steps
colourful make-up
red polka-dot shirt
slow erratic movements

Circus clown

ACTIVITY 6 Creating real people

- In this activity you are to **describe** the **characters** in the illustrations.
- Use your imagination to **provide clear word pictures**.
- Remember the **descriptive details** listed on the previous pages.

1 **Write** your **clues** here.

Now **write** your **description**.

The bushranger

2 **Write** your **clues** here.

Now **write** your **description**.

The trapeze artist

ACTIVITY 7 Creating real and 'unreal' people

Doctor Who is a very popular television series that has entertained millions of people since it began in the 1960s. The adventures of the Doctor (a Time Lord who travels through time and space) are still being watched today. Although the characters change from time to time, real *Doctor Who* fans never seem to mind.

Below are some brief notes describing one scene in the *Doctor Who* episode 'End of the World'.

- **Obtain** a DVD of this episode and **watch** it.
- **Use** the **notes** below to **create** a suitable **description** of **three** or **four** of the listed **guests**.

The guests

Doctor Who — black leather jacket — dark trousers — short cropped hair — wide smile
Rose Tyler — round face — shoulder-length blond hair — jacket — jeans
Three from the forest of Cheam — Jade, Newt, Coffer — strange creatures — reptile-like skin — flowing robes — padded shoulders
Grey blob-like creature — on round frame — elongated head — squashed body
The Repeated Meam — three dark figures — entirely in black
Brothers — grey reptile-like faces — tent-like cloaks — one orange, one brown — other two wicker head covering
Bird faces — tall — dark cloaks
Ambassadors — sharp pointed ears — distorted faces — red and orange cloaks
Huge head — wispy hair — enclosed in large glass container — wrinkled appearance
Cassandra O'Brien — last human — skin stretched on frame — arteries visible — two assistants — white

The guests

Descriptive scenes

When writing a **descriptive scene** you should describe aspects of the scene in an **order** that allows the reader to make a **complete picture**.

In the example below, the **first sentence** provides an **overall impression**. The following details allow the reader to visualise parts of the whole structure and gain a complete picture of the structure.

Example

The old barn

The old barn had seen much better days. A well-worn stone path led to a door in the centre of the front wall. One of its huge hinges was broken and the door was open at a rakish angle. The horizontal boards right across the front had patches of blistering paintwork here and there. The northern wall was leaning outward. It seemed as if an old gnarled gum tree was actually propping up this wall. The rusty corrugated iron roof was loose and some sheets flapped easily in the breeze. The once useful barn was now abandoned and almost beyond repair.

Task

Now **use** the picture below to **create** your own descriptive scene.

The tiny cottage

Descriptive scenes—time order

Sometimes a **description** needs to be **set out** in **time order** to provide an effective word picture.

The example below describes a scene as it unfolds in **chronological order**. The **first sentence** provides the **focus** of the scene. All the remaining details are provided in time order.

Example

Sundown at Bamfield

It was almost six o'clock. The sun was a golden ball in the west. Splashes of yellow could be seen on the waves far from the shore. The deep shadows were lengthening across the campsite behind the curved, sandy strip of beach. Soon the flocks of chattering lorikeets arrived to settle for the night. Gradually the colour of the sea darkened, as the sun sank lower and lower towards the horizon. At the campsite a few bright lights came on to disturb the evening shadows. Soon the sun was poised on the horizon. The peaceful ocean turned from dark green to almost black. Finally the sun slid below the horizon and darkness descended.

Task

Use the strip picture to create a description in **time order**. Use the **word clues** to help.

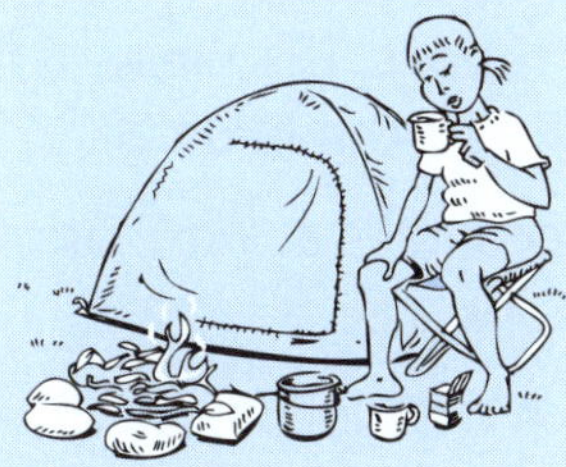

Clues

tinder dry twigs	brighter rays of sunlight	wisps of smoke
dry paper layers	flickering flame	wider, higher flames
heavier sticks	spurts of fire	drenched in sunshine

Part C **Focus on constructing texts**

In this section you will examine all the text types used in current syllabus documents. There are examples of each type and details of how to construct it, as well as a number of activities or writing projects so that you can practise.

9 Text types

In this chapter you will learn how to create the different **text types** you may be asked to write. They can be divided into two types:

- **factual** texts
- **literary** texts.

Factual texts

The main types of **factual texts** are listed below.

- **Procedure:** A procedure explains the steps or stages to follow to complete a task. It is set out so that the steps clearly indicate what has to be done.
- **Discussion:** A discussion is a text that looks at more than just one side of an issue or situation.
- **Explanation:** This answers the questions *how* and *why* in technical and scientific topics.
- **Exposition:** An exposition is a text that provides arguments for or against a particular view. It is a text that aims to persuade others to a particular point of view.
- **Information report:** This presents information on a particular topic, defining, classifying and describing it in detail.
- **Recount:** A recount is a text that tells us what has happened as a series of events. It can be factual or literary.
- **Description:** A description can be a stand-alone text or can form part of a larger text.
- **Response:** This is written to give a writer's feelings or attitude to another writer's views, or to a literary text, theatrical performance or artwork.

Literary texts

There are two main types of **literary texts**.

- **Narrative:** A narrative is a text that tells a story to provide information for the reader or to entertain.
- **Poetry:** Poetry was composed long before writing was invented. Poetry now can be in many different forms and is used for many different purposes.

Procedures

Procedures are texts that usually include:

- the **aim or objective** of an activity
- the **equipment and/or materials** needed to complete the activity
- a **number of steps** that must be followed in correct order
- **comment** on the result (optional).

Procedures will often include the following aspects of grammar:

- **action verbs**, **adjectives** and **adverbs**
- **phrases** telling us **how**, **when**, **where** and **why** introduced by prepositions.

Read this **science procedure**.

Example

Aim: to discover if plants give off water.

Equipment:

- a small plant
- four jars of the same size
- two sheets of paper
- 200 mL of water

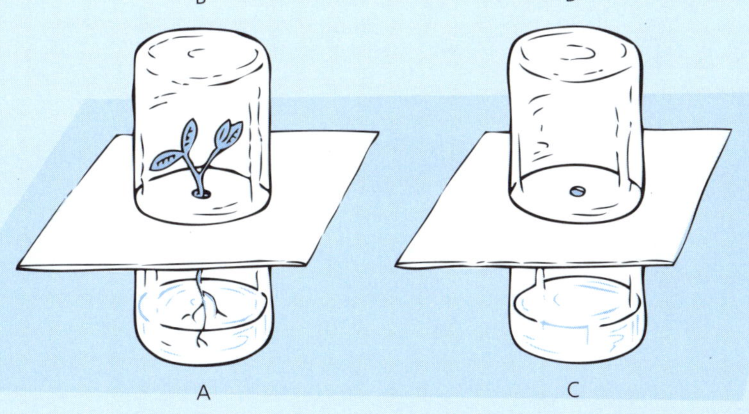

Steps:

1. **Pour** 100 mL of the water into jar A.
2. **Cut** a hole in one sheet of paper so that the plant leaves can be placed through the hole.
3. **Lower** the plant into jar A.
4. **Place** the paper over the plant and allow the leaves to poke through the paper into the upturned jar B.
5. **Pour** 100 mL of the water into jar C.
6. **Set** up jars C and D in the same way, with a sheet of paper (with hole) between them.
7. **Allow** jars to stand for fifteen minutes or so.
8. **Observe** the inside of jars B and D.

Comment/results: The jar with the small plant poking into it, jar B, will soon have droplets of water visible on the inside of it.

Note:

- Action words (verbs) are used at the beginning of each step.
- There are adverbial phrases such as the following:
  - *in the same way* (how)
  - *for fifteen minutes or so* (when)
  - *onto jar A* (where).

Procedures

Other types of procedures are written in the same way. Read this **mathematical game procedure**.

Example

The cover up game

Aim of the game: to be the first to cover up three adjacent numbers in a straight line—horizontally, vertically or diagonally—on the playing board.

Equipment: piece of cardboard 18 cm by 12 cm divided into rectangles (36 in all), three dice, green marker pen, twelve red counters, twelve blue counters

Steps:

- Enter numbers greater than 1 and less than 43 onto the game board in any order, for example:

16	19	11	4	26	32
8	14	31	42	2	19
11	23	26	3	39	10
38	18	6	13	7	22
33	25	28	40	21	17
9	24	34	27	35	5

- Mark one of the dice with the green marker.
- Give player A the twelve red counters.
- Give player B the twelve blue counters.
- Player A throws the three dice.
- Multiply the numbers shown on the plain dice and add on the number on the green dice. (If a player throws 6 and 3 with the plain dice and 4 with the green die the result is 6 x 3 + 4 = 22.)
- If the number 22 appears on the game board, player A covers it with one of his or her coloured counters.
- Player B now throws the dice.
- Player B multiplies and adds as before and if the number calculated appears on the game board it is covered with one of player B's coloured counters.
- If a player throws a number that has already been covered, it cannot be covered a second time.
- The game continues until one player has covered up three adjacent numbers in a straight line—horizontally, vertically or diagonally.

ACTIVITY 1 Writing a procedure—science

A writer prepared a text outlining the use of paper to support a book suspended between two jars. It was not written in correct procedure form. It did, however, have three useful diagrams in the text.

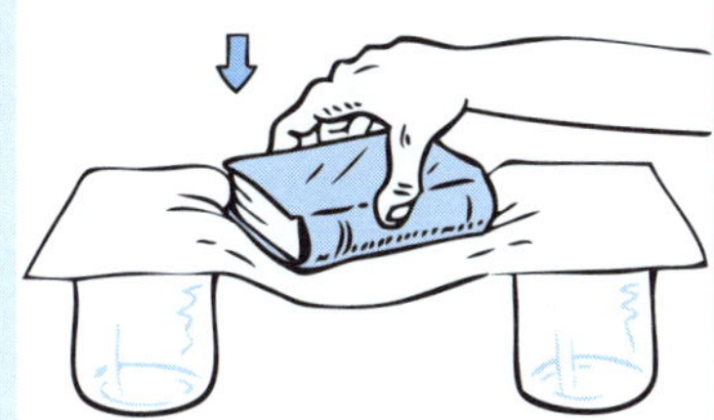

Firstly obtain two jars, two sheets of paper and a small dictionary. We need to find out if a sheet of paper placed flat between the two jars will hold the weight of a dictionary.

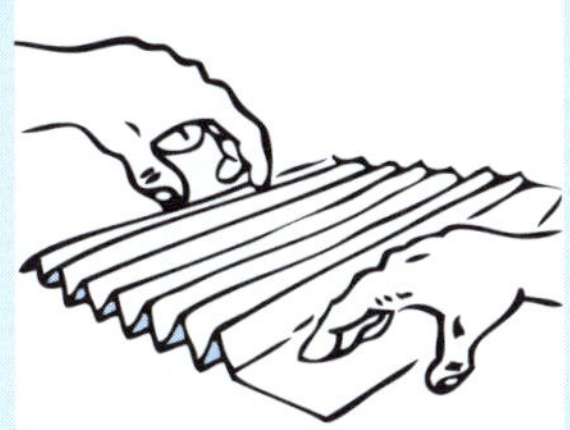

When the dictionary is placed on the flat piece of paper we notice that the paper cannot support the weight of the book and it falls into the space between the jars. If we take the second sheet of paper and fold it a number of times, we now have a 'corrugated' sheet of paper.

Then we can place the 'corrugated' sheet of paper between the two jars.

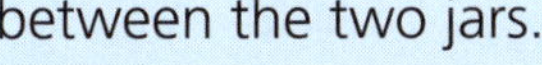

Now we place the dictionary onto the 'corrugated' sheet so the paper will support the dictionary.

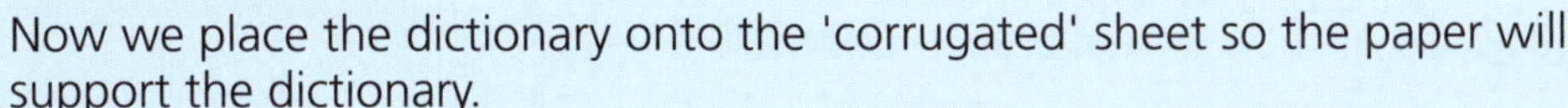

Read the text. **Study** the **diagrams** and then **rewrite** the text in **correct procedure form**.

Here are some **useful action words** you may need to use for this activity.

place fold move pleat collect allow lower set up

Aim: to show the strength of a single sheet of paper.

Materials:

Steps:

ACTIVITY 2 Writing a procedure—mathematical game

A writer prepared a text outlining the procedure for playing the Cave 100 game. It was not written in correct procedure form.

The aim of the game is to be the first person to reach the entrance to Cave 100. It has been designed for four players. You need a game card as shown below, two dice and a pencil. To begin the game the first player throws the dice and enters the total, say 9, above their name. The other players follow in the same way. After one throw the dice are returned to the first player. This player throws again (say 7). This is added to the 9 and the total 16 is written above the 9. The other players continue in the same way, taking turns to throw and add on to the previous total. The game keeps going until one player reaches 100 exactly. If a player reaches, say, 96 and then throws a number that makes the total over 100 they must remain on 96 until they reach 100 exactly.

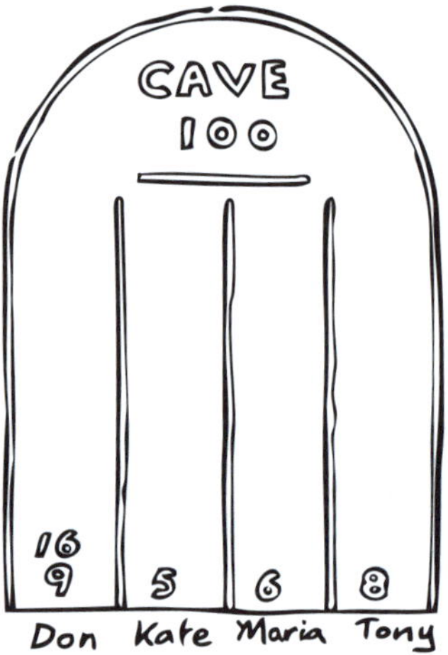

Read the text. **Study** the **diagram** and then **rewrite** in **correct procedure form**.

Here are some **useful verbs** you may need to use to complete the activity.

throw	add	enter	write
total	prepare	continue	complete

The Cave 100 game

Aim of the game:

____

____

____

Materials:

____

____

Steps:

____

____

____

____

____

____

____

____

____

Discussions

Discussions are texts that include:

- a **brief outline** of the issue or situation
- **arguments** for and against the issue or situation
- **evidence** supporting the various points of view
- a **conclusion** or recommendation.

Discussions will often include the following aspects of grammar:

- **extended noun groups** providing information
- **thinking verbs** that express the view of the writer
- **modal verbs** and **adverbs** (*might*, *must*, *possibly*, *probably*).

Example

Topic	Should homework activities be banned?
Brief outline	The issue of homework is one that has been written and spoken about for decades. For many years homework was regarded as essential for every student. Many parents thought that it was the duty of the school to provide homework activities. In more recent times there has probably been a shift away from this view.
Arguments for + evidence	Many students benefit from extra revision of daily work or extra practice at home. They have the opportunity to add to their skills by doing some of the same type of work done in class. In addition, students can work on assignments where they have to locate more information on a topic. This can be very useful if students make a good attempt to do their best. Evidence suggests that homework completed well does help the student make greater progress.
Arguments against + evidence	Many parents and students are not convinced of the value of homework. The twentieth century brought new forms of entertainment, and new types of households, which are also busier than in earlier times. Families in which both parents work and those with longer travelling times find it difficult to make time for effective homework. Normal family life is under greater pressure if students are burdened with long and complicated homework activities. In some cases homework is rushed and its value must be quite limited.
Conclusion	There is a case for keeping homework as part of a student's education. It should, however, be a limited amount so that the benefits of homework are not lost and time for normal family activities is not reduced.

ACTIVITY 3 Writing a discussion

The skateboard was a twentieth century invention. It is a fun and enjoyable way to get from one location to another. Expert skateboarders can perform amazing stunts but often risk serious injury in their pursuit of excellence.

The topic for discussion in this activity is:

Skateboarders should be barred from using their boards in shopping centre car parks. Discuss.

Read the notes **for** and **against**. **Add any others** of your own. **Use** the **introduction** provided and **complete the discussion**.

For	Against
danger to skateboarders from vehicles	skateboarders have few places to develop their skills
danger to shoppers from skateboarders	generally safer for skateboarders than using streets and roads
particularly hazardous to elderly shoppers	car park areas usually provide smooth, even surfaces
shopkeepers in centres may lose trade if some customers avoid centres that skateboarders use	can practise in areas where cars are not regularly parked

The skateboard, a twentieth century invention, provides adults and children with a fun way to travel short distances. The skateboard was developed from roller skates. It provides fun and excitement for huge numbers of people but skateboarders are usually not allowed in shopping centre car parks.

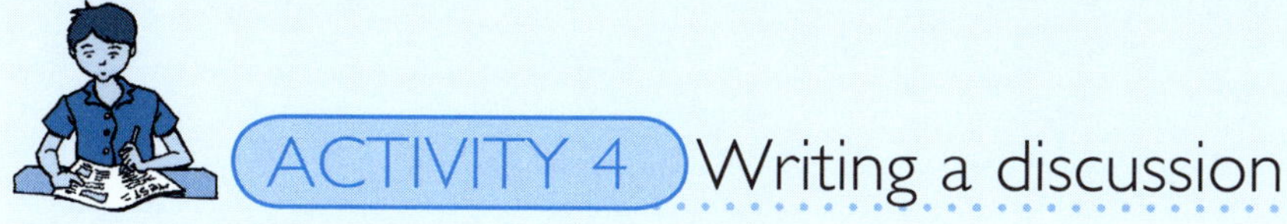

ACTIVITY 4 Writing a discussion

Here are **three topics for discussion**.

- Parents should set rules for Internet use on home computers. Discuss.
- People should be banned from camping in National Parks. Discuss.
- Should all shops be open 24 hours a day? Discuss.

1. **Read** each topic and **consider** the arguments for and against. **Jot** these **down** on a separate sheet of paper as you think of them.
2. After considering all three topics, **decide which topic** you would be able to discuss, bearing in mind the four aspects required for a discussion:
   - brief outline
   - arguments for and against
   - evidence
   - conclusion.
3. **Jot down** the **arguments for and against** in the table.

For	Against

4. **Write** the complete discussion.

Explanations

Explanations are texts that answer the questions *how* and *why* in technical and scientific topics. They include the following:

- **introductory statement** (what is being explained)
- **sequence of events**
- **conclusion** if required.

Explanations will often include the following aspects of grammar:

- **extended noun groups**
- **action verbs**
- **adverbial** and **adjectival phrases**
- **technical** and/or **scientific language**.

Example

Topic	How did horses develop?
Introduction	Some sixty million years ago the ancestor of the present-day horse first appeared. It has been called Eohippus and was no bigger than a fox. At that time, the continents were joined by land bridges and this animal moved about on all the continents of the northern hemisphere. Gradually, the animal grew stronger and larger, and it moved out from the undergrowth onto the plains. Once on the plains, these animals were in full view of their enemies. They had to learn to run faster.
Sequence	The original Eohippus had four toes on the front feet and three on the hind feet. It learned that it could run faster on its middle toe and tiptoe. Over many generations the remaining toes wasted away. The horse was left with one toe, the hoof of modern horses. All domesticated horses, regardless of their breed, are descended from the Eurasian wild horse. After the last Ice Age, some 10 000 years ago, there were two basic types of horses. Where the climate was temperate and the pastures lush, horses that were heavy, slow moving and placid developed. In harsher climates, finely built and faster horses developed. The heavy, placid horses thrived in the forests of eastern Europe. These became the heavy draught horses that were very valuable farm workers and carried armoured knights into battle. The more finely built and faster horses developed on the plains and open country.
Conclusion	The only true Ice Age horse that remains in much the same form today was discovered in 1881. It is believed that there are only forty specimens left in their wild state, although about one hundred are kept in various zoological gardens in Europe and America.

ACTIVITY 5 Writing an explanation

Some explanations rely on a flow chart or diagram to make the explanation clearer.

Read the **notes** below. **Discuss** the meaning behind the **illustrations**. **Prepare** an **explanation** on this topic:

How do eclipses occur?

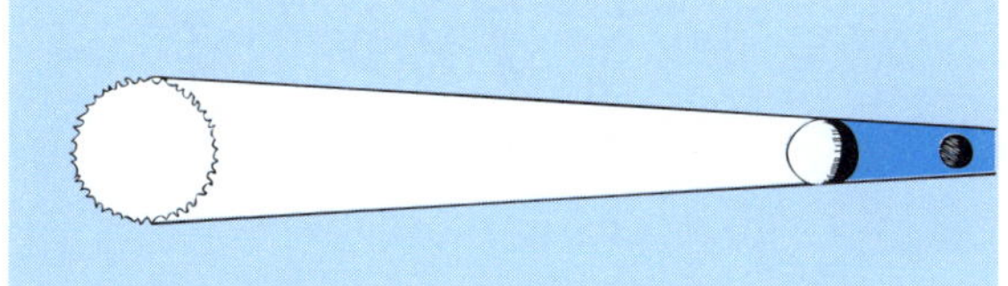

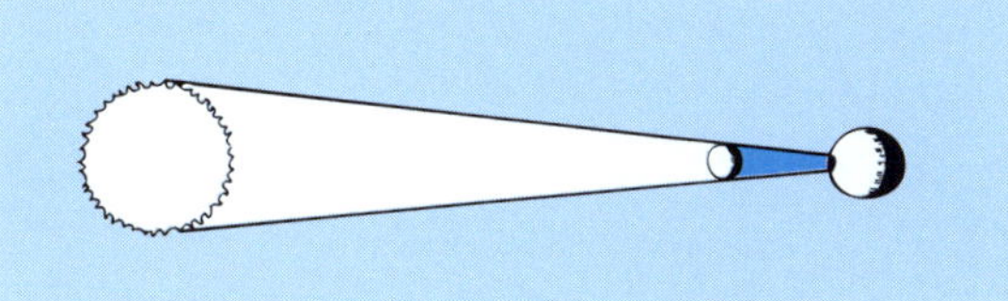

Notes

- the total or partial disappearance of the moon or Earth because of the shadow effect
- lunar eclipse — moon — into shadow of Earth
- solar eclipse — new moon passes between Earth and sun
- lunar eclipses — visible over large area of Earth — Earth casts shadow over moon
- solar eclipse — visible over smaller area — moon casts smaller shadow

ACTIVITY 6 Writing an explanation

How does your body use food?

Read the **notes** below. **Use** them to build the **explanation**. **Add** any other **information** to your work but make sure that the text you have added is correct.

- food — for growth, repair and energy
- growth and repair foods — protein — lean meat, milk products, eggs
- energy foods — carbohydrates, sugar, fats
- digestive system — mouth — oesophagus — stomach — small and large intestine
- protein digestion — starts in stomach
- protein, carbohydrates, fats — digested — small intestine — here — ready for use
- circulatory system — absorbs usable food into bloodstream — then to every part of body, every cell

Expositions

Expositions are texts that provide arguments for or against a particular point of view. They include:

- **introduction** (particular point of view)
- **arguments** and **evidence** (elaboration)
- **re-statement** of point of view.

Expositions will often include the following aspects of grammar:

- **extended noun groups**
- **action** and **thinking verbs**
- **modal verbs** and **adverbs** (*might*, *must*, *possibly*, *probably*).

Example

Topic	City bypass urgently needed
Introduction	The time for further discussion is over. There is an urgent need for a new bridge to bypass our congested city. It is urgently needed to prevent our city being choked by traffic. Why another bridge and access road? Other plans have been discussed, including widening the north-south arterial roads. To do this would be extremely costly. It would involve the resumption of many, many homes and businesses and the overall cost would be excessive. These other plans have met with much opposition. This is understandable. Any option other than a new bridge would involve huge delays and inconvenience. People do not believe any other solution is possible.
Arguments and elaboration	What is needed is a bridge approximately five kilometres west of the city. The through-city traffic creates gridlock conditions, particularly in peak hours. The positioning of a bypass bridge and access roads near Sexton Crossing is a very sensible plan. The river at Sexton Crossing is at its narrowest point for thirty kilometres. There are rocky cliffs on either side of the river. These would provide a suitable foundation for the bridge. Access roads north and south of the river would pass through undeveloped areas. There would be very little disruption to the life of the city.
Re-statement	It is important that planning begins immediately. It should be a priority for the council to undertake this significant bypass project as soon as possible.

ACTIVITY 7 Writing an exposition

All levels of government and many volunteer groups help provide activities for the young people of the community. There may be sporting venues and clubs that offer various art and craft activities, as well as game centres.

The idea of setting up Community Activity Centres for young people has long been seen as a way of encouraging them to participate in a wide range of educational and recreational activities. These could be set up by local councils and be open at weekends and school holidays. Many different activities, including indoor games, physical education activities, art and craft projects and computer skills programs, could be included in these Community Activity Centres.

In this activity you are to write an exposition on this topic.

Local councils should set up Community Activity Centres for young people.

The arguments for this proposal are that Community Activity Centres:

- provide fun, physical activities and learning experiences
- ensure that time is spent well and there is an absence of boredom
- are particularly useful during long holiday periods
- prevent situations where vandalism takes place because of young people having 'nothing to do'
- allow young people to make new friends
- aid physical fitness, as well as providing challenging learning situations.

Introduction	
Arguments and elaboration	
Re-statement	

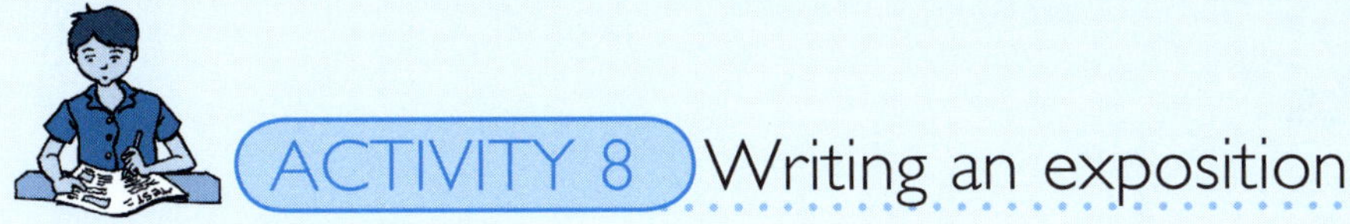

ACTIVITY 8 Writing an exposition

Here are three **topics**.

- It is an advantage to plant native trees and shrubs in our gardens.
- Governments should encourage and provide financial incentives to households to reduce water consumption.
- School canteens should only sell 'healthy' foods and drinks.

1. **Read** each topic and **locate** suitable **reference materials** on these topics. **Consider** the **arguments** for each point of view. **Jot** these **down** as you think of them.
2. After considering all three topics, **decide which topic** you would prefer to complete, bearing in mind that **three** aspects are required for the exposition:
   - introduction (point of view)
   - arguments and evidence (elaboration)
   - re-statement of position.
3. **List** the **arguments** for your position.

4. **Write** your **persuasive exposition**.

Information reports

Information reports are texts that provide information on a particular topic. Information reports include:

- a **general introductory statement** identifying the topic clearly
- **groups of sentences** providing information.

Information reports often include the following aspects of grammar:

- **relating** and **action verbs**
- **technical language**
- **paragraphs** organised to present information in logical sequence.

Example

Topic	Guinea pigs as pets
Introductory statement	Among the most popular of all domestic pets is the guinea pig. These tail-less rodents are descendants of the Peruvian cavy. They are particularly popular with children.
Groups of sentences	Guinea pigs are not intelligent animals and so they cannot be trained to follow commands or perform tricks as dogs do, but with gentle handling from an early age they can become very tame. However, loud noises make them nervous and they should be protected from them. Guinea pigs may be short haired, long haired, tan, gold, black, white, brown, albino, pied or brindle, or any variation in between. Guinea pigs, like all rodents, are quite prolific breeders, so care should be taken not to keep males and females in the same hutch unless you want to breed them. Hutches are easy to construct. They should have two compartments—a sleeping compartment free from draughts (as guinea pigs are susceptible to pneumonia) and an exercise run covered with strong wire netting. The base of the sleeping compartment should be covered with several sheets of newspaper and this should be changed every two days to keep the hutch hygienic. Straw, wood shavings or shredded newspaper makes ideal bedding for your guinea pigs. Move the hutch every day so that your guinea pigs have fresh grass to nibble. Guinea pigs eat fresh leafy garden vegetables, carrots, apple and even hard baked slices of bread. Provide them with fresh water daily in a spill-proof dish. You will find that having guinea pigs as pets is a rewarding experience.

ACTIVITY 9 Writing an information report

Use the **notes** in the box to **prepare** an **information report** on an area of Australia known as the Furneaux Islands. Refer to an atlas to locate the islands, which are at the eastern edge of Bass Strait.

Remember, an information report consists of:

- a **general introductory statement**
- **groups of sentences** providing **information**.

Furneaux Islands

Eastern end Bass Strait — Furneaux group islands. 1797 *Sydney Cove* wrecked — Preservation Island. Other explorers followed — sealers — whalers.

Furneaux Islands — remains of land bridge — Tasmania — mainland Australia.

Land bridge — appeared — disappeared — millions of years. Unique animals, plants — some extinct.

Sea birds — millions — huge colonies — isolated areas — gannets — largest rookery — Cat Island. Mutton birds — migrate — Furneaux group — fringe of Antarctic Circle.

Today — Furneaux group — windswept region — treacherous shoals — small settlements — farming — fishing.

ACTIVITY 10 Writing an information report

1. **Locate reference material** on the development of the great Persian Empire. The following points can be used as starters:
   - First settlers of Persia
   - Emergence of two powerful kingdoms in Persia
   - Expansion of the Persian Empire in the sixth century BC
   - Conquests of Cyrus the Great
   - Work of Darius
   - Decline of the Persian Empire
2. **Write** an **information report** on the Persian Empire.

ACTIVITY 11 Writing an information report

Throughout the world there are many endangered animals. *Endangered* means that such animals are in danger of becoming extinct.

Scientists believe that seventeen different Australian mammals have become extinct. Many other animals are also in danger of dying out.

1. **Locate information** using the Internet. See the website:

   http://www.kidcyber.com.au/topics/Austendangered.htm

2. **Prepare** an **information report** in your own words based on the details included in the website.

   Use the headings below:

   - Terms used to describe animals at risk
   - Reason for species being endangered
   - Examples and details of some of Australia's endangered animals

Australia's endangered animals

Recounts—factual

Recounts are texts that tell what has happened as a series of events. A **factual recount** sets out the series of events and summarises the importance of the events.

Recounts include:

- **information** based on the five Ws: who, when, where, what, why
- **chronological order** (in most recounts)
- a **summary statement**.

Recounts often include the following aspects of grammar:

- **action verbs**
- **adverbs** and **adverbial phrases** indicating time and place
- **adjectives** and **adjectival phrases**.

Example

Racing to the South Pole—Amundsen and Scott in 1911

By early September the winter was almost over and the temperature began rising steadily. Amundsen was becoming impatient. He knew that an English expedition under the command of Captain Robert Scott had arrived in Antarctica. The Norwegian leader was concerned lest the English expedition began the journey before his party could move out onto the ice. Amundsen and his party set off on 8 September but a sudden drop in temperature forced them to return. The temperature dropped to minus 50°C—the men suffered from frostbite, while the strength of the dogs was sapped by the extreme cold and their feet were cut and bleeding.

It was not until 19 October that the severe winter conditions had passed completely and the party could recommence the race for the pole. Amundsen selected four men—Hanssen, Wisting, Hassal and Bjaaland—with four sledges, each pulled by thirteen of the strongest and most reliable dogs. With good weather conditions, the party made good progress to the first and second depots as the dogs pulled the heavy sledges with ease.

After leaving the second depot, conditions on the ice deteriorated. The party entered a wild landscape of tall, white, glistening mountains with towering, bare cliff faces. Following the course of old glaciers, they reached a height of 1500 metres. Ahead were yawning crevasses, deep chasms and enormous blocks of ice. Day after day the huskies dragged the heavy sledges through this forbidding territory. At night, huddled in their sleeping bags in their frail tents, the explorers found their much needed rest was disturbed by the shuddering boom of avalanches.

Finally, the explorers had reached a height of almost 3500 metres and were entering a blizzard area. A depot was set up and twenty-four of the weakest dogs were slaughtered to provide meat for the remaining dogs and for the men. Fierce winds now slowed their progress and wild snowstorms and fogs reduced their visibility to a few metres.

The bitter winds continued as they crossed the Devil's Glacier—a wilderness with great blocks of ice barring the way. As they emerged from the glacier, they entered an area that Amundsen called the Devil's Ballroom. This relatively flat plateau had a thin, glasslike floor through which the dogs, men and sledges fell time and time again. Within a few days they moved out onto the plateau, with the South Pole only 160 kilometres away.

Almost immediately the weather began to clear and the ice surface was relatively flat and even. Certain of their goal, the Norwegians pushed ahead and, on 14 December 1911, reached their goal—the most southerly point of the globe.

A small silk tent flying the Norwegian flag was erected at the pole before the exhilarated explorers began the long return to base. Amundsen and his men had won the race for the South Pole.

ACTIVITY 12 Writing a recount—factual

The *Pandora* has historical links to the famous *Bounty* mutiny in the South Pacific. The *Pandora* was a ship sent out by the British Government to locate, apprehend and bring back to England any of the mutineers from the *Bounty*. The *Pandora* was wrecked in the far north of Queensland in 1791. It was on its way back to Britain with a number of *Bounty* mutineers who had remained on the island of Tahiti.

Use the **notes** below to **prepare** a **recount** on this **topic**.

The search for the *Pandora*

Arrange your recount in **four paragraphs**, according to the numbers.

1. Early searches
   - during late 1960s, early 1970s
   - difficult to locate
   - better search methods and equipment needed
2. John Hayer's research
   - with Steve Domm sailed from Cairns in the yacht *Reverie*
   - selected search areas
   - areas based on historical research
3. Ben Cropp and the *Beva*
   - Cropp — famous adventurer
   - helped in the search
   - carried out visual searches — no great success at first
4. Discovery
   - used magnetometer recording magnetic field
   - *Beva* marked out areas — November 1977
   - unsuccessful at first
   - by chance *Beva's* anchor — flat sandy area
   - large scatter of wreckage
   - cannons, parts of hull, iron stove, bottles, jars
   - certain to be *Pandora*
   - find reported to government

ACTIVITY 13 Writing a recount—factual

Here are three **topics**.

- Magellan and the circumnavigation of the globe
- The journey of Edward John Eyre across the Great Australian Bight
- The first man on the moon

1. **Locate reference materials** on these topics.
2. **Decide which** of these topics you would prefer to complete as a **factual recount**. Bear in mind that **chronological order** is important and that the recount should feature the following aspects:
   - preparation for expedition
   - personnel and mode of transport
   - summary of main events in chronological order
   - results of expedition.
3. **Write** your factual recount.

Recounts—literary

Recounts are texts that tell us what has happened as a series of events. A **literary recount** tells a story as a **sequence** of events.

Example

The dare

It was almost dark! The time Sven had been dreading had arrived.

Earlier in the day he had boasted to his friends that he was game to enter the dam pipes, any time, any day—some boast.

The huge dam stood across the narrow Nelson Valley. When the valves were opened thousands of litres of water would rush through the pipes every second. Nobody was stupid enough to climb up into the pipes, but Sven had said that he would.

Sven crept out the back of the house and down to the spillway of the dam. His friends were waiting. The dark, menacing pipes were above their heads. Sven could not escape. To be looked on as a fool or a coward would be a great hurt.

The weather had turned cold and Sven was shivering, but not just from the cold, he thought. How long were the pipes? Did they finish under the dam wall? What was at the end of the pipe? What if they turned on the valves? The thought made him shiver even more.

Slipping his lucky charm under his shirt he climbed up to the entrance of the pipe on the right-hand side. Rounding the corner of the spillway path, he could scarcely see for the shadow cast by the wall.

His breathing was coming a little faster but, clenching his teeth, he knelt at the opening and ran his hands around the smooth pipe. The sweat was starting to mark his shirt but on all fours he began to enter. No other form of darkness could have prepared him for this.

Advancing slowly with hands outstretched, he crawled along. He had to continue straight on. The slime in the pipe forced him to proceed even more slowly. He counted the crawling steps he took—ten, twenty, thirty, forty. It seemed like hours but he thought it must only be a few minutes.

Then his trembling hand reached what he thought was a heavy steel grate. He could go no further. He'd done it!

Trembling with relief he began the return journey backwards. Soon he was able to breathe the fresh, clean air outside. 'Never again,' he thought out loud, but with a smile of satisfaction on his face.

ACTIVITY 14 Writing a recount—literary

Below is the beginning of a **literary recount**. Note that the introduction **sets** the **essential details** for the rest of the recount:

- personnel
- time
- location
- initial activity.

Read the first part of the **literary recount**. **Consider** the characters and activity they are engaged in and then **complete** the **literary recount**.

Trouble at the crossing

Young Jed Adams was an assistant to a horse-team driver. His master, Matt Henderson, was a kindly man, but one who demanded that his young helper do his best with the work. Backwards and forwards from Sydney to small western country towns, Jed and Matt and their twelve-horse team would travel. Carrying wool or farm produce to Sydney and returning with food supplies and farm equipment was their regular task. Early one Tuesday morning in July 1838, Jed attended to the horses and, with a heavy load of wool, they set off on the rough road back to Sydney. Much rain had fallen lately and washouts were common.

At the top of Preston's Hill, Matt brought the horses to a stop. The steep, downhill section of the road was badly rutted and slippery.

Suddenly before

Descriptions

Descriptions can be stand-alone texts or can form part of a much longer text.

- Descriptions of **people** often include:

height	build	eyes	hair	skin	clothing	footwear
distinguishing marks		expressions		gestures	general attitude	

- Descriptions of **scenes** should first provide an **overall impression**. Additional details allow the reader to **visualise** parts of the whole scene and **build up** a **complete picture**.

Descriptions are made up of:

- an **introductory statement** of identification
- **groups of sentences** providing detailed descriptions.

Descriptions often include the following aspects of grammar:

- **extended noun groups**
- **adjectives** and **adjectival phrases**
- **adverbs** and **adverbial phrases**.

Examples

The old sailor

Beside a tumbled collection of stained tubs and barrels stood a tall, thin man with his curly, brown hair almost hidden by a faded blue cap. His narrow face was deeply lined and his widely set dark blue eyes gazed out across the water. A thin scar stretched from the far corner of his left eye to his top lip. A bushy, dark brown moustache beneath a hooked nose and a tight-lipped mouth completed his serious and weather-beaten face. As we approached, the old sailor clambered to his feet and came towards us. His face broke into a crooked smile and his stained and broken teeth were clearly visible.

The harbour view

The harbour at Port Kennedy presents a tranquil scene on a calm day. Looking from the top of Milman Hill directly south, we can see the timber and concrete navy wharf extending about 60 metres into the clear, blue water. A grey, sleek-looking navy patrol boat is tied up at the wharf as young children fish from one edge. To the south-west is the main wharf, its shiny concrete reflecting the sun and providing good shelter for the trawlers and other vessels that are clustered around. Forklift trucks scurry along the wharf to the main shed where goods are stored. In the sheltered cove next to the main wharf, small dinghies bob up and down on the slight swell. Our eyes move across the front of the town, over the powerhouse, to see a white vessel come into view. Its skipper carefully judges the approach to the wharf and, slowly, the ship is moored safely. Several men begin unloading general cargo onto a white truck parked on the wharf next to the ship.

ACTIVITY 15 Writing a description

Notes are given for two topics. The first is a description of an individual, the second a description of an object.

Select one topic and **use** the notes to **write** a **description**.

male — about 190 cm tall — solid build
straight red hair — ponytail
bright brown eyes — angry stare — long scar on left cheek
ragged T-shirt — board shorts
tattoo of ship on right forearm
no shoes — lounging near entrance to dock

commemorative decoration
150 years Norfolk Island settlement by Pitcairners
mid-brown cut-out shape of island
all coves and bays
top section — rough piece of tanzanite — slight glow
brilliant gold rectangle
blue stones — ocean — diamond — sun
dates 1856–2006 clearly displayed

Responses

Responses are texts that are written to give a writer's **feelings** and **attitudes** to literary texts. There are two different types of response: personal responses and reviews.

Personal responses include:
- **introductory background** identifying text and subject
- **personal opinion** of writer to other writer's text.

Reviews include:
- **introductory background** and identification of characters
- **general description** of text
- **opinion** or **judgement** of the work.

Responses often include the following aspects of grammar:
- **persuasive language**
- **expanded noun groups**
- **verb forms**.

Example

An article in the *Daily News* made the following points in relation to water supply.
- Water charge to householders will treble within three years.
- The cost to manufacturers will mean that goods will be much dearer to produce.
- Local industries that use large volumes of water will relocate to other areas where water costs are cheaper.
- Costs for additional, urgently needed water storage will further increase costs to households and businesses.

A **personal response** to this article follows.

Central theme: water crisis and increasing costs

I read with interest the article regarding increasing costs for water in the area. The unfortunate fact is that councils and governments have failed to build new water storage facilities. The seriousness of the situation is clear. Our district cannot afford to lose the industries that have been established here. It would lead to a loss of jobs and would affect the whole economy of the region.

Urgent action is needed now. Households should be encouraged to install tanks and all new homes should be required to have at least 20 000 litres of water storage capacity. All households must begin recycling grey water to use in gardens.

The dangers of not doing anything are real. Minimise water use and build additional water storage facilities now. Costs of water can be limited if enough action is taken now.

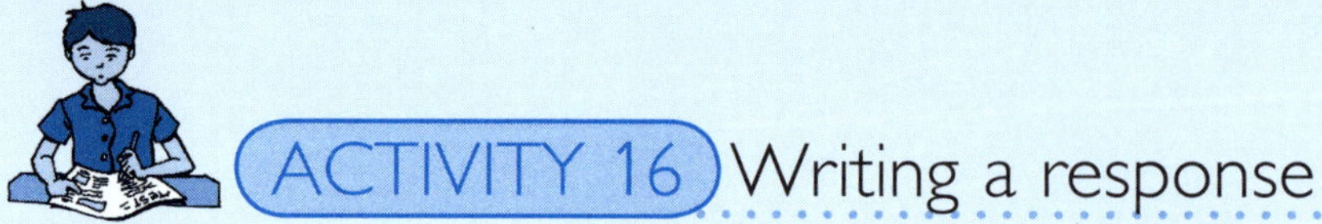

ACTIVITY 16 Writing a response

1. In your local newspaper **locate several short articles** or **letters to the editor**. **Read** these carefully to decide whether you **agree** or **disagree** with the central theme in each one. **Share** your ideas with other students. **Prepare** a short list of all the **arguments for** or **against** the central themes.

2. **Respond** to **one** of the articles or letters. **Note** the **central theme** and **supporting details**.

   Central theme: ______________________________

   Supporting details: ______________________________

   ____

   ____

   ____

3. Using the details above, **create** a **response**.

   Response:

Responses—reviews

A **book review** is a particular type of **response**. It includes **introductory background** and **identification** of the **characters**, **setting** and **theme**. It also includes a **general description** of the text and an **opinion** or **judgement** of the work.
Reviews may be **set out** in a number of ways. They include:

- **title of book**
- **reviewer's name**
- **author of book**
- **characters**
- **setting**
- **events**.

Example

Name of book: *E Day and Counting*, by S. Catteral

Name of reviewer: Sandy Malouf

Author

The author Sean Catteral is well qualified to write a book detailing the problems of our ecosystems. For many years he has travelled to areas of the world where density of population is causing severe environmental damage. He has written many magazine articles showing the exploitation of natural resources caused by excessive immigration to particular areas. Much of his life has been devoted to studying the problems of overpopulation and congestion in cities, towns and waters.

Overview

The author reports on damage to a number of significant areas. In particular, his research on and discussion of the Amazon basin of South America, the enlargement of the desert areas of Africa and the emerging problems of many of the world's waterways make interesting but disturbing reading.

Details

Each of these three major areas receives detailed attention. In the chapter on the Amazon basin he reveals that the extent of logging and burn off is so severe as to imperil whole species of flora and fauna not found in other areas of the world. The indigenous people, who for centuries have lived in relative harmony with this magnificent area, are now threatened with the total loss of their way of life. His tables of population and areas of erosion and land degradation clearly indicate an environmental catastrophe. The fact that every indigenous community is at risk is highlighted in his discussion.

The chapters on the gradual expansion of the African deserts and the consequences of overgrazing and poor land management show a problem of massive proportions. In the final three chapters photographic and scientific evidence is presented to show the enormous scale of pollution of waterways.

Conclusion

This book again clearly shows the problems of overpopulation and environmental vandalism. That the author provides few answers to the problems highlights the need for further research.

ACTIVITY 17 Writing a response (review)

In this activity you will keep a list of the books you have read during the year and prepare a review of a book that you enjoyed a great deal.

1. As the year progresses, **list** the **books** you **read** in the table below.

Books completed	
Name	Author

2. When you have **decided** on the book you enjoyed the most, **prepare** a **review** of it. **Revise** the headings that you will need to use by **looking at** the sample on the previous page.

Review of ______________________

Narratives

Narratives are texts that tell a story to **provide information** for the reader or to **entertain**. Narratives include:

- **orientation** introducing main characters, time and place
- **complication**—the sequence of events that causes a problem for the main characters or others
- **resolution**—the detail that explains how the complication is resolved
- **coda**—an optional aspect that identifies any discoveries or learning that the incident has provided for the main characters or others in the narrative.

Example

The hospital visit

It was Saturday morning and Greg was not in good shape. All week he had suffered from a shoulder problem he had gained the previous Saturday when he played half-back for his team, the Wanderers.

Now it was aches and pains all over. It seemed like the flu and Greg always hated feeling sick.

Should he go to the hospital? he thought. The only medical service on the weekends was at the hospital. He put off making a decision, but as the morning went on he felt worse.

By eleven o'clock he could wait no longer. Despite his dislike of doctors' waiting rooms and hospitals he set off on his new Ducati.

As he sat in the crowded room occupied by fellow sufferers he thought of the fishing trip he was missing. Time passed slowly, ever so slowly.

Finally a nurse appeared and led him to a small room. Once again he waited. After a wait of twenty minutes the nurse returned. Greg's patience was almost at an end. The nurse apologised for the delay but explained that the regular medical staff were attending an emergency at a nearby homestead. She also explained that a medical student from out of town would see him soon.

Greg, inwardly fuming, sat and waited—ten, twenty, thirty minutes. At last the medical student arrived. After preliminary conversation a thermometer was placed in Greg's mouth and the student left.

Once again, time passed—ten minutes, twenty minutes—this certainly wasn't Greg's day.

Incensed by the delays, Greg stormed from the room, past the group waiting in the foyer. Down the corridor was the student engaged in discussion with the nurse.

Greg restrained his impatience, passing the thermometer to the student. The student then proceeded to turn his back on Greg and, holding the thermometer up, appeared to discuss the reading with the nurse.

Now completely at the end of his patience, Greg turned to the student. Stabbing his index finger at the instrument he stated loudly. 'I'll tell you! When the silver line gets to here you're in big trouble.' And he stormed off. He felt better already!

ACTIVITY 18 Writing a narrative

1. The notes below form a **skeleton outline** for the beginning of a narrative entitled *The Rescue*. **Use** this beginning to **prepare notes** for the **remainder** of the narrative.

Notes: The Rescue

Mark, Ali, Noela — four wheel drive — beyond Cloncurry.

Vast plain — rugged hilly — outcrops — blazing sun.

Left beaten track — ascending — steep rocky incline.

Suddenly engine stalled — balanced crazily — one moment — lurched sideways.

Vehicle rolled over twice — Mark thrown clear — Ali, Noela injured — unconscious.

Carefully — removed — shady tree.

Then ______________________________

2. **Use** the notes to **create** an **interesting narrative**.

Poetry

Poetry is written in many different forms and can be used for many different purposes. A poet is one who is able to express thoughts in musical and memorable language. Some of the many different types of poetry are:

- **narrative poems** (telling a story)
- **ballads** (telling a story, usually about a dramatic or important event)
- **descriptive poems** (describing poets' experiences of the beauty of this world).

A very common type of narrative poem has the following features:

- **four lines** per verse
- **rhyming words** at the end of the second and fourth lines
- four **accented syllables** in the first and third lines, and three accented syllables in the second and fourth lines.

Example

Otto Snell

Come, list to me and you shall hear
A tale of what befell
A luckless lad of Clifton town—
His name was Otto Snell.

From day to day he swung a pick
With right good manly zest,
A brawny youth was he who went
Two metres round the chest.

When freed from toil, his greatest joy
Was but to find some lout
Who'd undertake a round or two
At a willing boxing bout.

It chanced one day a seeming 'dude'
Arrived at Clifton town.
'Ah here's a chance', thought Otto Snell
To take this dandy down.

A contest at the local Hall
Was presently arranged,
Could Snell have had a prophet's sight
His tune full soon had changed.

For when the combatants had stripped
Poor Snell was sore amazed,
The 'dude' exposed a well knit frame
That Conan might have praised.

The fight began, but Otto's pals
Soon gave up all their hopes,
'Round Two' beheld their champion stretched
Half lifeless on the ropes.

With outstretched hand the 'dude' advanced
Said he, 'It's rather late
To introduce myself but I'm
Toowoomba's Heavy weight.'

P.W.R.

befel = happened
zest = enthusiasm
brawny = strong
lout = rough youth
dude = well-dressed, polite person

ACTIVITY 19 Writing poetry

Complete the following short poems with suitable **rhyming words**. When you have finished, **check** that there is a **consistent rhyme scheme** and that the pattern of **accented syllables** is consistent throughout.

1 **Rhyme** lines 2 and 4.

The sun

I saw the sun on the ocean blue
Its fingers rose from the morning d _ _ .
It lit the world with its bright array
To work along throughout the d _ _ .

2 **Rhyme** lines 1 and 2, and lines 3 and 4.

Butterfingers

Butterfingers lets things f _ _ _ ,
Doesn't matter large or s _ _ _ _ .
Anything he tries to t _ _ _ ,
He's always sure to drop and b _ _ _ _ .

Lots of eggs he's sure to s _ _ _ _ ,
And if you hear a great big c _ _ _ _ ,
Which sounds just like a breaking c _ _ ,
Butterfingers is washing u _ !

When he tries to play a g _ _ _ ,
It always happens just the s _ _ _ .
Every time the catches s _ _ _ ,
From his quite unsteady g _ _ _ ,
The other players stand and s _ _ _ _ ,
Butterfingers you are o _ _ !

3 **Rhyme** lines 1 and 2, and lines 3 and 4.

The toy machine

Fourteen hours of solid w _ _ _
I drive along without a j _ _ _ .
I cannot play around all d _ _
I move the factory on its w _ _ .

All day I have so little f _ _
As there is work I haven't d _ _ _ .
I give to children so much j _ _
With each and every brand new t _ _ .

At night I have a little r _ _ _ ,
And children by whom I am truly b _ _ _ _
Lie tucked in bed so very t _ _ _ _ ,
While moonlight shines on me so b _ _ _ _ _ .

ACTIVITY 20 Writing poetry

Below are details of three short forms of **poetry**.

- **Read** the examples and **consider** how they have been created.
- Then **write** an **example** of your own.

Cinquain

A **cinquain** deals with one experience, detail or idea. The form is:

- **1st line**: title (1 word)
- **2nd line**: description of title (2 words)
- **3rd line**: action of title (3 words)
- **4th line**: feeling about title (2 words)
- **5th line**: synonym for title (1 word)

Example

Gymnast
supple, agile
twisting, balancing, turning
capturing attention
beauty

Your cinquain

Haiku

Haiku is a traditional Japanese form of verse, telling about one particular impression or experience. The form is:

- **1st line**: 5 syllables
- **2nd line**: 7 syllables
- **3rd line**: 5 syllables

Example

The snow is falling
Soon the winds begin to blow
Swirling, swirling round.

Your haiku

Limerick

A **limerick** usually has a humorous or nonsense theme. The form is:

- **1st line**: 3 stresses
- **2nd line**: 3 stresses
- **3rd line**: 2 stresses
- **4th line**: 2 stresses
- **5th line**: 3 stresses

Lines 1, 2 and 5 rhyme and so do lines 3 and 4.

Note that Americans call autumn *fall*.

Example

There was a young feller named Hall,
Who fell in the spring in the fall.
It would have been a sad thing,
Had he died in the spring,
But he didn't, he died in the fall.

Your limerick

Answers

Answers have not been included for extended writing projects as students' responses will vary greatly. A teacher or adult should check the answers to these activities.

1 How to write narrative and factual texts

Page 7 Activity 1

(Sample answers) Karl, Karen Currie — twins — eleven years old — love horses — helping around the farm — dog Rover — good working dog children own — Arab ponies — Tewala, Michelle — favourite ride to Longlands Gap crossing — six kilometres away from homestead — set out before eight o'clock — took water bags, fruit — muesli bars — riding ranges — steep slope — snake frightened horses — reared up — riders crash down slope — injured — Karl hurt sprained ankle — broken arm Karen — unconscious — Karl tore part of shirt — tucked into dog's collar — shouted at Rover to go home — long hot wait — blazing sun — hardly a breath of wind — Karl listened carefully — suddenly sound of engine — parents — utility — rescue — urgent attention to injured children

Page 11 Activity 3

Paragraph 1, line 3: capital letter on *Because*
Paragraph 2, line 1: full stop after *trip* and capital letter on *They*
Paragraph 4, line 3: capital letter on *Victoria*; correct spelling of *Sydney*
Reposition paragraph 6 as paragraph 5; reposition paragraph 5 as paragraph 6
Paragraph 7, line 1: correct spelling of *mapped*

2 Making and using notes

Page 15 Activity 1

(Sample answers)
Third expedition: most difficult — Geraldton — Murchison River — Robinson Ranges
Dangerous country: water shortage — found two springs — Weld and Wendich Springs — sand and rock wasteland — terrible heat — salt lakes
Result: government — realised area unsuitable — settlement

Page 17 Activity 3

(Sample answers)
English longbow: made of one piece of wood — yew the best — about 1.8 metres long
Value of the longbow: large numbers of bowmen — helped win battles — Crecy — Agincourt
Skills: needed strength — practice — need string, arrow — pull back, aim and release — one action
Using the longbow: hold string by first three fingers of right hand — leather guard for fingers — bracer prevents grazing — good bowman twelve arrows per minute

Page 19 Activity 5

(Sample answers)

Key words	Notes
Bears	many countries — mostly northern hemisphere — strongly built — thick coats — flat, wide feet — long, strong claws — good sense of smell
Brown bears	found in Europe, Asia, North America — North America — Grizzly — Kodiak largest — 2.8 m high — 700 kg
Black bears	Himalayan black bear — 1.5 m high — 100 kg — Asia — mountainous regions — Sun bear — Asia
Polar bears	Arctic region — difficult to see on ice and snow — good swimmers, divers
Food sources	Plant and animal food — insects, fruit, wild honey — some eat meat, fish, 'omnivorous' feeders

Page 20 Activity 6

(Sample answers)

Key words	Notes
Australian Wildlife Conservation	main aim — conservation Australian wildlife — begun 1991 — founder Martin Copley — set up Karakamia — West Aust. — now 12 properties — 600 000 hectares
Set-up	controls on feral animals and weeds in place — threatened animals reintroduced
Endangered animals	high rate of extinctions — fifty endangered species — threats foxes, feral cats — competition goats, rabbits
Karakamia	south of Perth — 9 km vermin-proof fencing — 260 hectares fenced prevents foxes and feral cats — many species reintroduced — woylie, numbat, quenda, Tamar wallaby, quokka, Western Ringtail possum

Answers

Example	sanctuary shining example — 100 different birds — 24 reptiles — 9 frog species

Page 21 Activity 7
(Sample answers)

Key words	Notes
A. B. Paterson	born 1864 — eldest of 7 children — grew up NSW
Early years	sent to Sydney Grammar School — ten years old — lived with grandmother — became articled clerk — qualified as solicitor in 1886
Writing tasks	began writing poetry for *Bulletin* — 'Banjo' very popular poetry — 'Clancy of the Overflow', 'The Man from Ironbark', 'The Man from Snowy River' — wrote verses, stories — country experience — war correspondent — Boer War — Great War
Other works	lived in Sydney — wrote — published several children's books — broadcaster for ABC — 1939 received award — service to literature — died 1941
Appeal of work	exciting yarns, comic situations — incidents — courage — mateship — love of country

4 Punctuation and writing conventions

Page 39 Activity 1

1 **a** Jack, Michella, Andy, July **b** Tuesday, Brad, Tina, Neilson **c** During, April, Reverend G. L. Ashton, Ford **d** The, Altandi Street, Sunnybank, Clarkson Road **e** The, Ellison, Wanaka River, Toronto Gulf **f** The, Jenolan Caves, Blue Mountains, Sydney

2 **a** Mt Everest, Tibet–Nepal, A, Everest, Lhotse, Nuptse, The; full stops after *frontier*, *Nuptse*, *direction* **b** Roald Amundsen, Oslo, Norway, July, As, Sir John Franklin, North-west Passage, By, Belgica, Antarctica; full stops after *1872*, *passage*, *Antarctica* **c** After, Battle, Zama, Punic War, At, Romans, The, Carthaginian Empire, Hannibal; full stops after *ended*, *additional 20 000*, *Hannibal*

3 (Sample answers) **a** Jenny, Cape Byron, New South Wales **b** Avondale, Tara **c** James Transport, Lennox Head, Melbourne **d** Miah, Bass Strait **e** Cathy, Philomena, Lyric, Hamlet

Page 41 Activity 2

1 **a** old, broken, yellow **b** young, frisky, brown **c** pelicans, ducks **d** Alan, Marco, Guiseppe, Alex **e** Atherton, Mt Garnet, Cairns, Cooktown **f** three o'clock, six o'clock, nine o'clock

2 **a** ✓ **b** ✗ The soldiers attacked quickly, quietly **c** ✗ My eldest brother, Adam, **d** ✓ **e** ✓

3 **a** E **b** Q **c** E **d** Q **e** E, E

4 **a** slipping! **b** Ouch! **c** here? **d** books? **e** mess! **f** machine?

Page 43 Activity 3

1 **a** can't **b** hasn't **c** o'er **d** o'clock **e** they'd **f** who've **g** it's **h** you'll **i** baby's cry **j** women's coats **k** tigers' tails **l** gentlemen's hats

2 **a** these farmers' crops **b** the man's wife **c** several teachers' classes **d** these birds' nests

3 **a** ladies' **b** friend's, girl's **c** monkeys', horse's **d** fishermen's, stranger's **e** acrobat's (S) *or* acrobats' (P), town's **f** friend's, cousin's

4 **a** items: **b** substances:

5 **a** basket; **b** sound;

Page 45 Activity 4

1 **a** pit-a-pat **b** stick-in-the-mud **c** nine-tenths **d** anti-war **e** sea-legs **f** round-up g bird-table **h** clear-cut **i** ninety-nine **j** stake-out

2 **a** jet-black **b** light-hearted **c** well-prepared **d** co-ordinators **e** anti-whaling

3 **a** —fifteen months to be exact— **b** —temperature as high as 35°C— **c** —pottery, painting, sculpture, collage, work and screen printing **d** —kilometres from any civilisation—

4 **a** (founded in the USA) **b** (already a winner in the singles) **c** (more than one hundred of them) **d** (see page 36 of the manual)

Page 47 Activity 5

1 **a** ✗ forty-nine **b** ✓ **c** ✓ **d** ✓ **e** ✓ **f** ✓

2 **a** four metres **b** 0.003 mm **c** forty-five square metres **d** ten minutes

3 **a** 3 September 2009 *or* 03.09.09 **b** 9.45 p.m. **c** 3.07 a.m. **d** 9.32 a.m. **e** 10.10.08 (alter year as appropriate) **f** Tuesday, 17 January 2006

Page 49 Activity 6

1 **a** Qld **b** Wed. **c** para. **d** Col. **e** fem. **f** NT **g** incl. **h** cert. **i** WST **j** Dec. **k** adj. **l** SA

2 **a** Aust. **b** ETA **c** esp. **d** deg. **e** EDP **f** fol.

3 **a** anon. **b** Co. **c** fwd **d** bal. **e** sing. **f** excl. **g** approx. **h** etc. **i** long. **j** recd

4 **a** *Répondez s'il vous plaît* (French for *Please reply*) **b** On Her (His) Majesty's Service **c** central business

Answers

district **d** United Nations International Children's Emergency Fund **e** annual general meeting **f** non-English speaking background

Page 51 Activity 7

1 **a** 'When will you be able to finish it?' the supervisor asked.
b 'No,' she said, 'I will not collect the parcel.'
c 'Look,' cried the boy, 'you have broken it!'
d 'Come on,' said John, 'it needs to be done quickly.'
e The young girl whimpered, 'I know I've lost it.'

2 **a** indirect **b** direct **c** indirect

3 (Sample answers)
a 'Where have you been?' asked the teacher.
b He said that he had not done it.

4 **a** The traveller said that he had never been to Lake Eyre before.
b The old timer explained that the hills, especially in the north, were very steep.

5 (Sample answers)
a 'Which is the way to the post office?' Maddie asked the tall stranger.
b 'We are going to the football,' some of the children announced.
c The teacher explained, 'The divisor in the operation is twenty-three.'

Page 52 Activity 8

1 **a** 'Will you follow the track?' asked Jim. 'It's a long way but the scenery is beautiful. Look out for snakes on the way.'
'I certainly will,' replied Jay.
b An employer was interviewing a young lady and had almost completed his discussion with her. Finally he said, 'Do you have any religious views?'
'Well,' said the girl, 'I can't say I have, but I do have some good pictures of Sydney Harbour and Luna Park.'

2 **a** donkey's tail **b** girls' dresses **c** boy's marbles **d** workmen's jobs **e** princes' coats **f** mother's books

3 (Sample answers)
a Tom said to Jack, 'I am going to collect his books before nine o'clock on Saturday.'
b 'I am planning to travel to Armidale during the May vacation,' Evan said to John.

4 **a** 'Where do you think Fairdale is located?' enquired the salesman.
b 'Did Carol and Michelle read the book "Sea Rescue" during the May holidays?' asked the librarian.
c 'Have you ever heard the band play "St Louis Blues"?' asked the soldier.

5 Writing better sentences

Page 53 Task

1, 3, 2, 3, 2

Page 54 Task

(Sample answers)

1 Many young animals of various sizes grazed there.
2 The talented girl with long dark hair became a pianist of world standard.
3 The entertaining magician gave the boy from interstate a rabbit with pink ears.

Page 55 Task

(Sample answers)

1 Several birds were seriously injured by the vehicles.
2 The boys effortlessly painted the fence during the day.
3 Then the young girl climbed the hill without delay.

Page 56 Activity 1

(Sample answers)

1 The kind stranger in uniform happily gave the visitor a fifty-cent coin at once. *or*
The delighted stranger in grey work clothes hastily gave the visitor a fifty-cent coin early in the day.
2 The weary boys in ragged clothes hungrily ate the food after three o'clock. *or*
The famished boys in uniform ravenously ate the food with great speed.
3 The hard-working farmer with a beard soon found the bags near the chaff-cutter. *or*
The experienced farmer with work-worn hands reluctantly found the bags after much searching.
4 Cheerful students in school uniform excitedly left the school before lunch. *or*
Excited students over eight years old hastily left the school at once.

Page 57 Task

(Sample answers)

1 His favourite pastime developed over many years was trail bike riding.
2 The girl enjoyed weight training with her friends.
3 Running is a great hobby enjoyed by many people.

Page 58 Task 1

(Sample answers)

1 The car to be repaired is by the shed.
2 The artists to complete the project gathered in the lobby.

Answers

Page 58 Task 2
(Sample answers)
1 The animals waiting at the gate ran away. *or*
The animals to be bandaged ran away.
2 The girl wearing a blue dress arrived. *or*
The girl arrived to celebrate her birthday.
3 The worker entering the building enjoyed the machinery. *or*
The worker fixing the old machines enjoyed the machinery.

Page 59 Task
(Sample answers)
1 The students who had come from interstate played.
2 The car that had been along the track appeared.
3 The visitors toured the park while the parents arranged the ceremony.

Page 60 Activity 2
(Sample answers)
1 a The convenience shop on the corner had been painted recently
b The well-worn carpet behind the sofa was stained badly.
c This green trunk was found to be very heavy.
2 a Several animals with thick coats crept through the jungle at dawn.
b The man in the green coat sold the products during the week.
c The range with the rocky cliffs is impossible to climb in the rainy season.
3 a Many of the exhibitors enjoyed planning their displays.
b The young girl walking to the shop entrance is a good friend of mine.
c All the animals to be treated for the infection were kept in a separate room.
4 a The young lady who lives in Armidale is my niece.
b All the animals will be transported away when the show is over.
c The celebrity who came from Sydney presented the trophy to the winner because she was impressed by the work.
d If it is found, the mountaineer's gear, which was lost in the storm, will be packed carefully.

Page 61 Task
(Sample answers)
1 After studying the map, Sue travelled along High Street, turned down Jane Street and finally reached Sandra's house.
2 Max found the rabbit, which had escaped, where it was hiding near the shed and carried it back to the owner.
3 When the brilliant white car arrived, they admired it, as did many others who came to see it.
4 The travellers were very cautious and took extreme care, as the track was very steep and dangerous with loose rocks.

Page 62 Task
1 a Through the narrow opening the tiny creature that had been trapped now cleverly escaped.
b Now the tiny creature that had been trapped cleverly escaped through the narrow opening.
2 a Towards the abandoned cabin the escapee, injured by the fall, crawled through the darkness at dusk.
b At dusk, the escapee injured by the fall crawled through the darkness towards the abandoned cabin.
3 a Close to the fireplace, the beautiful tawny Abyssinian cat curled itself up and immediately fell asleep.
b Curling itself up, the beautiful tawny Abyssinian cat immediately fell asleep close to the fireplace.
4 a Almost blanketed by the dense fog, the riders increased speed on the downhill run.
b On the downhill run the riders, almost blanketed by the dense fog, increased speed.

Page 63 Task 1
1 There, There, They, There, They, There (There, They)
2 Many, Young, Sitting, It, Others

Page 63 Task 2
Laura, She, Laura, She, She, Laura, She (Laura, She)

Page 64 Activity 3
(Sample answers)
1 Allan and Rod were enjoying a holiday with their aunt and uncle, whom they had begun visiting many years ago. The boys really enjoyed the holiday cottage where they often left early in the morning to explore the coves and caves. Often they spent all day on the beach and around the cliff. Watching the sun go down from the back deck was something they always enjoyed.
2 Sanchia and her friends had decided to go camping on Friday Island. On a fine day, with the sea very calm, they set out with their camping gear in their small outboard. After reaching the island, which was only eight kilometres from their home, they secured their boat and carried the gear ashore. Their first task was to decide on a suitable campsite. After checking several areas they found a sheltered spot and carried all their gear over to it. Nearby were a fresh water spring and a large swimming hole.

Answers

Page 65 Activity 4

(Sample answers)

1 When Jason went to the produce store in the village he bought some food for the pony and a new halter.

2 After Sharon found the box in the lunch room she took it home, where she showed it to her parents.

3 **a** At the centre many of the animals that had been injured in the fire were treated carefully by the wildlife personnel.

b Carefully, the wildlife personnel at the centre treated many of the animals that had been injured in the fire.

4 At nine o'clock the visitors arrived at the zoo, where they lined up in a long queue. Within twenty minutes they were inside the main gate so they took the opportunity to enjoy a cup of coffee before studying the map of the zoo. All of them wanted to look at the new polar bear enclosure so they decided to go there first. The distance to the enclosure was only three hundred metres.

Page 66 Activity 5

(Sample answers)

1 **a** skilful, in the red suit **b** golden, from overseas

2 **a** in the evening, quickly **b** soon, strongly, from the east

3 **a** to paint the fence **b** playing tennis **c** smashed badly **d** to collect carefully

4 **a** with a red roof, which won the rally **b** of exotic flowers, that I borrowed from the library

5 **a** <u>during</u> the afternoon, <u>when</u> the track became even steeper **b** <u>if</u> you complete the work, <u>before</u> the end of the week

6 **a** carefully, yellow, by Aunt Clara **b** green, favourite, who came across the mountain

Page 67 Activity 6

(Sample answers)

1 As the explorers entering the ranges had journeyed for weeks, their supplies, which were running low, needed to be replenished.

2 **a** Into the ranks of the defenders fired the group of archers who had boldly turned to the right of the castle wall.

b Turning to the right of the castle wall, the group of archers fired into the defenders' ranks.

3 The labourers, coming early with their equipment, knew it would be a long day. To complete the drainage trenches in the hard-packed earth would be difficult. Beginning immediately, they soon felt beads of perspiration running down their backs but they continued. After three hours they had a break from their task.

6 Paragraphs

Page 69 Activity 1

1 End first paragraph *mist*; end second paragraph *world*

2 End first paragraph *energy*; end second paragraph *distances*

Page 70 Task 1

Paragraph A: 1, 2, 4, 5, 7, 9; Paragraph B: 6, 11; Paragraph C: 3, 8, 10, 12

Page 70 Task 2

(Sample answers)

A: 1, 2, 4, 5, 7, 9; B: 11, 6; C: 10, 3, 8, 12

Page 71 Activity 2

(Sample answers)

1. Squash has become a very popular sport in Australia. In squash, racquets and a hard rubber ball are used. The game of squash is an indoor one, a little like handball. The players use racquets to hit the ball against any of the four walls of the court.
2. In the 1960s an international federation of countries playing squash was set up. Many countries agreed to play according to international rules. Nine countries, including Australia, joined the international federation.
3. Heather Blundell displayed great skill at hockey, tennis and squash. Heather won the junior and senior titles at the age of seventeen. Heather went on to become one of the greatest female squash players of all time.

Page 72 Task

A: 1, 6, 3, 2, 4, 5; B: 1, 4, 6, 2, 3, 5

Page 74 Activity 3

1 Many different types of sport were practised in England during the Tudor period of history. (Type A)

2 The African slave trade was one of the most inhuman and shameful activities in which many countries participated. Conditions were harsh and cruel and the countries involved were condemned for their role in this terrible example of inhumanity. (Type B)

3 Madame Marie Curie, born in Poland, became a great scientist and was honoured by most countries for her work on the discovery of radium. (Type A)

4 It was in 1956 that Herb was inspired with a fierce determination to become one of our greatest runners—it was a turning point in his life. (Type C)

Answers

Page 75 Activity 4

1 In the Olympic Games the longest race of all is called the marathon.

2 As he stood there in the bright sunlight, this powerfully built man was an impressive sight.

3 Christopher Columbus, the son of a weaver in Genoa, became the greatest sailor of his time.

4 The main vessel used by Columbus when he discovered the Americas was the *Santa Maria*, the most famous carrack of all.

5 One of Australia's greatest champion racehorses was Bernborough. *or* Bernborough, through his great ability and will to win, became a racing legend.

Page 76 Activity 5

1 The quarter horse is probably the youngest breed of horse in America. *or* Some people think that the quarter horse can do more jobs better than any horse in the world.

2 The Caribs and Arawaks lived on the islands of the West Indies for centuries.

3 The dangers of a climb to the top of Mt Everest are immense. *or* On the top slopes of Everest, the temperature can drop to minus 40°C. Without effective and reliable cold-weather protective clothing, survival in this hostile environment is impossible.

Page 77 Task

In 1827 Captain James Stirling had explored the Swan River area of Western Australia and regarded it as ideal for settlement. Supporting details: reported to English government; Thomas Peel set up group to colonise; wanted to settle 10 000 persons; 1829 Captain Fremantle took possession; Captain Stirling soon after selected sites of Perth, Fremantle for settlement

Page 78 Activity 6

1 The Portuguese, Dutch, English and French traders were keen to establish trading centres in India and the East Indies. Supporting details: Portuguese first to find sea route to India; Dutch began rich trade in spices from East Indies; 1600 English East India Company set up; trading at Surat, Madras, Bombay, Calcutta; French began trading at Pondicherry; rivalry between English and French led to war

2 One of the most famous car designing salons of the last fifty years is the workshop of Nuccio Bertone near Turin in Italy. Supporting details: created beautiful shapes for many years; greatest designs in Lamborghinis, Ferraris, Lancia Stratos; earliest creations Alfa Romeo and other sports cars in 1950s–1980s; other car companies used Bertone salon (BMW, Volvo); English manufacturers also used

Page 83 Task

1 Of all the apes these are the most attractive. (B)
Many gorillas have been badly treated in circuses over the years. (A)
Many other animals do this as well. (A)
Gorillas must be the most intelligent of any animal in the animal kingdom. (B)

2 Good eyesight is very important for driving at night. (A)
The aperture of a camera is very similar to the pupil of the eye. (C)
It is possible to have cornea transplants these days. (A)
The retina is much the same as the film in a camera. (C)

Page 84 Task

1 'Quickly close the door behind you', whispered Mary urgently as she moved past the table.
'What on earth for?' asked Toni in a puzzled tone and she walked towards the open door.
'I just heard someone outside, or at least I'm pretty sure I did', replied Mary.
'Oh, you are just imagining things again', answered Toni with a smile on her face.

2 'I'm afraid I lost my favourite Labrador dog a few days ago', said Sam in a sorrowful tone.
'Well', said Sarah, 'why don't you put up notices around the area or an advertisement in the newspaper?'
'Probably wouldn't do much good', answered Sam. 'I never did get around to teaching him to read.'

3 'That new driving instructor you hired for me is terrible', Louise said in a dejected tone.
'Why do you say that?' asked husband Tim, surprised by his wife's comment.
'Well, today he nearly killed me three times with his silly advice when I was driving', replied Louise.
'Oh, come on, dear', the husband replied. 'Why don't we give him one more chance?'

7 Setting a scene

Page 87 Task

1 **a** lake **b** cathedral **c** skirt **d** photocopier **e** volleyball **f** warder **g** thistle **h** blues

2 (Sample answers) **a** lake **b** semi-trailer **c** sausages **d** bread **e** floorboards **f** flowers **g** saxophone **h** envelopes **i** jar **j** unleaded petrol **k** zebra

Answers

Page 89 Activity 3

(Sample answers)

1 parents, Jan and Thomas, lemon, capsicums, picker, a grasshopper, insect
2 Buck, Mitre, moths, apricot, shed, canoe, Wilson family
3 cousins, months, hide and seek, boots, teepee, bikes and scooters, cleared area, volleyball
4 lion, thicket, front paw, antelope, veterinarians, field, woman, dart gun

Page 90 Task

(Sample answers)

1 **a** damaged window, tractor shed **b** younger brother, palm tree **c** heavily-built man, metal box **d** decorated cake, polished table **e** bronze coins, clean counter

2 **a** The huge road train travelled along the Alison Highway.
b The young boy Aaron followed the long-haired German shepherd.
c The fast flowing Eudlo Creek flowed through Mooloolah Valley.
d The cheeky lorikeet flew to the flower-laden grevillia shrub.
e On the sparkling computer desk was a rare Chinese dish.

Page 91 Activity 4

1 **a** The most sheltered forest in Erin valley was shrouded in fine mist. ✓
b The grey-haired old man was chopping the huge pile of dry wood. ✓
c The spirited young Arabian pony galloped across the wide training yard. ✓
d The speeding yellow Ford had been repaired at the modern well-equipped workshop. ✓
e The excited family took a short trip to the newly opened zoo. ✓
f Many small Persian kittens played happily in the fur-lined basket. ✓
g All along the crowded busy street the tiny mopeds travelled quickly. ✓
h The tall steel building shone brightly in the early morning sun. ✓
i Many of the colourful lorikeets in the area rested in the tall, stately pines. ✓

2 (Sample answers)
a Jason and his elder sister Paula went to the brilliant rock concert.
b The young actor, Ethan Adams, waited at the narrow door to the brilliantly lit stage.
c Joseph's cousins Lisa and Svetlana enjoyed the film *Beowulf*.
d The large passenger liner was sailing through the narrow, dangerous strait.
e The shiny, plastic water pistol was used to amuse the Anderson children.
f Apples, pears, potatoes and onions were collected by the young backpackers.

Page 92 Task

(Sample answers)

1 advance **2** dart **3** strike **4** ridicule **5** attain **6** award

Page 93 Activity 5

1 **a** skipped **b** snatched **c** struck **d** stomped **e** shaking **f** rushing **g** tumbled **h** jumped
2 **a** crouched **b** glared **c** eased **d** lingered **e** snarled **f** crashed **g** hurled **h** sneaked **i** smashed
3 (Sample answers) travelling, roared, reached, began, applied, smashed, splashed, escape from
4 (Sample answers) **a** amble, stroll, trudge, advance **b** shout, yell, scream, whisper **c** devour, chew, digest, chomp

Page 94 Task

1 **a** ambled **b** whistled **c** trotted **d** scrambled **e** spurred **f** slammed **g** charged **h** nudged **i** hopped **j** blurted
2 **a** sobbed uncontrollably **b** interrupted rudely **c** grumbled quietly **d** struggled wearily **e** rumbled loudly **f** trotted proudly **g** waddled awkwardly **h** advanced carefully

Page 96 Activity 6

1 **a** (ii) They had been playing for almost an hour inside the new shed. For several hours rain had been falling and the narrow path was covered with water. They hurried along the side of the building to stack their game equipment in the rows of boxes near the doorway.
b (ii) Within a few minutes the group had entered the narrow cave. In the stillness they could just hear the bubbling sound of water softly cascading down the rock face within metres of the entrance. Using torches, the group lit their path as they began the dangerous descent of the narrow moss-covered passageway, which snaked down to the silent rock pools below.

Answers

Page 97 Activity 7

(Sample answers)

1 **a** Yesterday several of the workers began moving the rubble from the building site. Broken bricks, stones and smashed pieces of timber littered the area. The actual site was located at Glennie and had been used as a dump for several years. Within two days the largest items had been removed. These had been taken to the refill site by huge dump trucks.

b Mid-morning came and the heat beat down mercilessly. The travellers were in the Ellenral Plateau and the huge boulder-strewn plateau was a terrible obstacle to the weary group. By midday the lack of water created additional hardship. At three o'clock they had reached the mid point of the desolate border region. Overcome with weariness, they rested at Devils Marbles for two hours. Setting out again, they realised that they had sufficient food for only the next three days.

8 Creating word pictures

Page 102 Task

1 **a** sound **b** smell **c** sight **d** taste **e** touch **f** sound **g** sight

2 (Sample answers) **a** dark, forbidding **b** ancient, stone **c** priceless, modern

Page 104 Activity 2

1 **a** (ii) taste **b** (ii) smell **c** (ii) sound **d** (ii) sight **e** (i) touch **f** (i) sight

2 (Sample answers) **a** bright, clear **b** sudden, terrifying **c** sweet, overpowering **d** rich, chocolate **e** heavy, rough **f** towering, majestic **g** booming, thundering **h** burnt, scorched

Page 105 Activity 3

1 sleek, four-masted; small, densely forested; gleaming first rays; tropical; snaking from a campfire; well-armed; small golden stretch of beach; palm; white-tipped swells; wild figure; clad in ragged clothes of goatskin; long matted hair and beard

Page 106 Task

1 boredom **2** disappointment **3** love or affection **4** happiness **5** anger **6** fright **7** pride **8** agony

Page 108 Task

1 **a** as swift as a gazelle **b** as white as snow **c** like thunder **d** as playful as a kitten **e** as hungry as a lion **f** like tufts of golden wool

2 **a** cat was a delightful bundle of excitement **b** trees were ghostly shapes **c** vessel was a silver galleon **d** sun was a golden shaft of light **e** mountains were jagged pyramids of shining rock **f** decorations were a writhing mass of colour and movement

3 (Sample answers)

- **a** The tiny bird was a fluffy bundle of colour. (metaphor)
- **b** The large white tent was a great comfort for the exhausted travellers. (metaphor)
- **c** Some of the art works were as valuable as the Crown jewels. (simile)
- **d** My young cousin is as strong as a horse. (simile)
- **e** The fighter aircraft was a blinding silver blur. (metaphor)

Page 109 Task

1 (a) and (c) **2** (a) and (b) **3** (a) and (d) **4** (a) and (c) **5** (a) and (d) **6** (a) and (d)

Page 110 Task

1 (b) **2** (b) **3** (a) **4** (b) **5** (a)

Page 111 Activity 5

1 (Sample answers)

- **a** The tiny dog was a mischievous ball of curly white hair with two black tipped ears.
- **b** My sister wore a sparkling red costume covering her thin, tanned body.
- **c** Many of the runners wore light coloured clothing and high quality cross trainers.
- **d** Some fine ponies decorated with colourful bridles moved proudly around the show ring.

9 Text types

Page 148 Activity 19

1 dew, day

2 fall, small, take, break; smash, crash, cup, up; game, same, slip, grip, shout, out

3 work, jerk, day, way; fun, done, joy, toy; rest, blest, tight, bright

Notes